the cheese course

the cheese course

Enjoying the World's Best
Cheeses at Your Table

CHRONICLE BOOKS
SAN FRANCISCO

JANET FLETCHER
photographs by Victoria Pearson

Acknowledgments

Because this book has, in all the best ways, been an educational process for me, I must thank the many cheese authorities who have been my teachers. With gratitude for their advice, serving ideas, and recipes, I would like to acknowledge the following: Kate Arding and Sue Conley of Tomales Bay Foods; chef Rodger Babel; Kate Collier of the Cheese Works Ltd.; Judy Creighton of Creighton's Cheese and Fine Foods; chef and longtime friend Hallie Harron; Greek food authority Lidia Kitrilakis; cheese enthusiast and dear friend Roberta Klugman; chef Heidi Krahling of Insalata's; Joyce McCollum and Richard Tarlov of the Oakville Grocery; Greek cheese importer Jeanne Quan; Cakebread Cellars chef Brian Streeter; Paula Wolfert; and Daphne Zepos. For their guidance on wine with cheese, I would like to thank Tim Hanni, Nick Peyton, and Shirley Sarvis. For her encouragement and suggestions in the preliminary stages, I thank Linda Sikorski of the Pasta Shop. I also am deeply grateful to Janet Tarlov of the Oakville Grocery and David Zaft of the Pasta Shop for reviewing the manuscript. Finally, my thanks to editor Bill LeBlond and all the folks at Chronicle Books for allowing me to share my enthusiasm for cheese with a wider audience.

Text copyright © 2000 by Janet Fletcher; photographs © 2000 by Victoria Pearson.

All rights reserved. No part of this book may be reproduced in any form without written permission from the publisher.

Library of Congress Cataloging-in-Publication Data:

Fletcher, Janet Kessell.
The cheese course: enjoying the world's best cheeses at your table by Janet Fletcher; photographs by Victoria Pearson.
p.   cm.
Includes bibliographical references and index.
ISBN 0-8118-2541-8 (hc)
1. Cookery (Cheese) 2. Cheese. I. Title.

TX759.5.C48 F58 2000
641.3'73 21—dc21   99-046593
CIP

Printed in Singapore.

Prop styling by Ann Johnstad
Food styling by Christine Anthony-Masterson

Designed by Shawn Hazen

The photographer wishes to thank Owen Masterson, food stylist assistant; Jon Nakano, photographic assistant; AIM Color Lab; and the Beverly Hills Cheese Shop.

Distributed in Canada by
Raincoast Books
8680 Cambie Street
Vancouver, British Columbia
V6P 6M9

10 9 8 7 6 5 4 3 2 1

Chronicle Books
85 Second Street
San Francisco, California 94105

www.chroniclebooks.com

page 2: *fresh sheep's-milk ricotta with peaches and pistachio-currant biscotti, page 76.*

contents

enjoying the cheese course

As a college student spending a semester at a university in France years ago, I think I learned more out of the classroom than in it. At farmers' markets, in restaurants, and at my host family's table, I saw how much time the French put into preparing and enjoying their main daily meal.

In homes and in restaurants, I came to love that moment when the cheese tray arrived, when the glasses would fill with wine again and the pace of the meal would slow. Out would come more bread and a basket of fruit. Over a platter of local cheeses or a wedge of Camembert, the conversation would pick up, the day's pressures would be forgotten, and I would find myself wishing that the meal wouldn't end.

Back home in California, I began serving a cheese tray, too, drawing on the limited selection at local shops. I loved the way it stretched out a meal, especially with friends around. And I liked the communal nature of it, as people shared from a single platter. But even at weekday dinners, with just my husband and me at the table, I would put a cheese or two out at the end of dinner to provide an excuse to sit awhile longer.

"It's the only course that gets better the longer it sits in front of you," says Nick Peyton, a San

Francisco restaurateur and cheese enthusiast. "The cheeses temper [come to room temperature]. The wine opens up. There's nothing to get hot or cold, melt or coagulate." A cheese course offers the promise of unhurried pleasure.

For twenty years now, I've been serving cheese enthusiastically, inspired by those memories of France (which I've renewed several times since). But over the past few years, I've noticed my options expanding dramatically. We Americans are clearly in the midst of a cheese revolution, with dozens of American cheesemakers reviving the craft on an artisanal scale, and with cheese imports exploding. Importers are bringing in European cheeses unavailable just a few years ago, such as artisan Toma from Italy's Piedmont region, a remarkable array of Tuscan pecorinos, and cheeses from Spain—such as Afuega'l Pitu, Mahon, and Zamorano—that I had frankly never heard of.

Every time I visit the best cheese shops near my Napa Valley home, there are new arrivals, new tastes. As I write this, a merchant has just called to tell me about the Australian farmstead cheeses his store is importing. What a wealth of choice we have today.

And the revolution isn't only at the cheese counter. American restaurants have also begun to take cheese seriously, adding cheese courses, cheese aging rooms, even staff cheese specialists, as at Picholine in New York. In the old days, if I saw cheese on a menu, I thought, "Why bother?" The selection was invariably mundane and straight from the fridge.

No longer. At restaurants around the country, chefs are presenting cheese in enticing ways. In fact, this book began to take shape in my mind when I noticed their efforts to make the cheese course more inviting. By adding a special nut bread, a complementary salad, or perhaps a chutney or fruit compote, these chefs could seduce people into ordering cheese who normally wouldn't. At the same time, I noticed that the clerks at one of my favorite cheese shops were urging me to buy a few glazed figs to put on my cheese platter or a wedge of Spanish dried-fruit cake or a slice of quince paste.

Call it merchandising on their part, if you like, but I found these recommendations so appealing that I thought perhaps a small book of such ideas would persuade more people to bring cheese home for their own table. I have no illusions that a cheese course will soon be the daily habit in America the way it is in some homes in France, but I do believe that I might make some converts to the practice of serving a single cheese with a salad at the end of a family dinner, or a platter of cheeses with an unexpected accompaniment at the end of a dinner party, in lieu of dessert.

There is much to celebrate in this country's rapidly growing interest in cheese. Not only does it threaten to make us slow down our meals—hooray for that—but it also rewards the dedicated artisans who are preserving cheeses of long tradition and creating new cheeses of distinction.

purchasing cheese

If you are eager to buy and serve good cheese, you'll need the help of a knowledgeable merchant. Sadly, few of America's supermarket chains have "bought into" cheese. Most supermarkets carry only predictable, factory-produced specimens, cut and wrapped, with no one available to offer tastes or advice. (Not that you'd want to taste those lifeless cheeses anyway.) To its credit, the Whole Foods chain is a high-profile exception, with an extensive selection of cut-to-order cheeses and a trained staff. Maybe its success will influence others.

In the meantime, you may need to go out of your way to find well-chosen and well-cared-for cheeses. Here are a few things to look for.

> SELECTION: A large selection is nice, but a thoughtful selection is even better. I like to see a merchant supporting local producers and small-scale artisans. I also look for cheeses identified as "farmstead," meaning they are produced from the maker's own herd. These cheeses are rare, and certainly many of the world's finest cheeses are not farmstead. Instead, the cheesemaker buys the milk from the best local sources. (In fact, some would argue that freeing cheesemakers from animal husbandry allows them to concentrate on their craft.) When you shop for cheese, note whether the merchant offers interesting choices you don't see everywhere. Does the selection include any raw-milk cheeses, which usually have more flavor than their pasteurized counterparts? (Due to U.S. regulations, only cheeses aged more than sixty days can be made with raw milk.)

> APPEARANCE: How does the cheese display look? Do any cheeses look dried out, moldy, sweaty, or poorly wrapped? Is the case a jumble, or is it neat, organized, and well signed? "If the cheese is displayed well, that tells me the people like the product they sell," says David Zaft, a cheese authority who works for the Pasta Shops in Oakland and Berkeley.

> KNOWLEDGE: Look for merchants who care enough about what they're selling to educate themselves and their staff. Can the clerks tell you which blue cheese is the mildest or—to start from the start—what kind of milk the cheese is made from? Can they suggest accompaniments or cheeses to complement the one you've chosen? Do they volunteer descriptions or information about the cheeses?

ENTHUSIASM: At the cheese shops I admire most, I rarely have to ask for a taste. If I peruse the selection for more than a minute, a clerk will begin offering samples, pointing out new items and asking questions about what I'm seeking. It's worth going out of your way to buy from people who are passionate about cheese. They will teach you something every time you buy. In return, I try not to monopolize a clerk's time, especially at rush hour, and to make my decision promptly.

SERVICE: Are cheeses cut to order, or are most items precut? Once cheese is cut and exposed to air, it begins its decline. Plastic wrap hastens that decline by trapping moisture and imparting an unpleasant taste. When possible, buy from a store that cuts cheese to order and wraps it in heavy waxed paper or something other than plastic. If you have to buy precut cheese, check the wrap date to make sure it's no more than a couple of days old.

Even if you don't have a helpful merchant, you can educate yourself. Make it a habit to buy an unfamiliar variety each time you shop for cheese. It's all too easy to reach for your favorites, but if you regularly seek out the ones you don't know—perhaps even keeping a tasting notebook—your knowledge will grow.

With the exception of hard cheeses such as Parmigiano-Reggiano, pecorino romano, and aged Cheddars, I try to buy only as much cheese as I expect to use in the next few days. Some types will last much longer if properly stored (see Storing Cheese, page 17), but they don't improve. And once their container is opened, some fresh cheeses are more perishable than milk. Try to buy ricotta, fromage blanc, mozzarella, or mascarpone the day you intend to use it, or no more than a day or two ahead.

serving cheese

With a few exceptions that you'll note in the following recipes, I prefer to serve cheese at the end of a meal. I do enjoy a few thin slices of Manchego or Dry Jack with warm olives (page 91) before dinner, or marinated bocconcini (page 25) as a first course with summer tomatoes, or a cheese tray as the main event at a picnic. And on a slow weekend morning, some runny Bellwether Farms' Crescenza with raisin toast (page 26) would suit me fine.

But I'm not a fan of the American custom of serving a cheese tray with drinks before dinner. Cheese is rich, and hungry guests are likely to overindulge and ruin their appetites. I would rather serve the cheese platter after the main course when appetites are somewhat sated.

On the other hand, I have learned over the years that if I want my guests to enjoy the cheese course, I need to make sure they are still a little hungry when it is served. When I plan to serve cheese, I make main-course portions modest.

planning your cheese platter

1. Choose an appropriate tray.

Select a platter or tray roomy enough for your guests to have easy access to each cheese. You might use a rustic wooden board; a wicker or silver tray lined with edible leaves, such as grape or fig leaves; a marble or granite cheese board; or a small piece of unfinished marble or granite.

For serving several cheeses, I purchased a large, round wicker tray and had a glass insert made for it. The glass lifts out and cleans easily. I must say it is impressive when brought to the table, but it's cumbersome to pass. I'm coming around to the idea that it's often better to put two cheeses on one tray and two on another. The smaller trays are easier to pass and the service goes faster.

2. Don't serve too many cheeses.

It's easy to be seduced at the cheese counter, but try to hold yourself to three or four choices. Most palates can't handle more than that without tiring. Besides, an enormous cheese tray tends to stop conversation as guests try to make their way through it.

As this book amply demonstrates, even one cheese can constitute a pleasing cheese course if it's carefully chosen and attractively served.

3. Aim for variety.

Select your cheeses with an eye to diversity in appearance, texture, milk source, and flavor.

APPEARANCE: Visualize the shapes and colors on the platter as you make your selection. If you buy a round of Munster, then add a wedge of Stilton and a pyramid or log of goat cheese. If you choose a chalky-white goat cheese or a pale ivory pecorino, add visual contrast with a rich gold Dry Jack or the deep orange Shropshire Blue. A cheese wrapped in chestnut leaves, coated with herbs, or covered with ash can also add eye appeal.

TEXTURE: Contrast moist, creamy cheeses with firm, dry ones. Pair an unctuous triple-crème Explorateur with an aged Gouda, for example. Juxtapose a silken, buttery Taleggio with a chalky Coach Farms goat cheese pyramid.

MILK SOURCE: Vary your guests' taste experience by offering a cow's-milk, a goat's-milk, and a sheep's-milk cheese.

FLAVOR: Seek cheeses that offer a range of flavor profiles, from mild to pungent.

Don't feel bound by these guidelines, however. It can be fun, for comparative purposes, to serve cheeses that have something in common—perhaps three goat cheeses of varying age, or three cheeses from Spain, or an English Cheddar and a Vermont Cheddar.

4. Bring cheeses to room temperature.

At least two hours ahead, take cheeses out of the refrigerator. If the pieces are large, take them out even earlier. Flavor and texture are at their best when the cheese is at room temperature. Never, never serve cold cheese.

5. Provide appropriate implements.

If possible, accompany each cheese with its own knife to prevent flavors from intermingling. Hard cheeses will need a sharp knife or a cheese plane. Small butter knives are fine for soft, spreadable cheeses. If you don't have enough knives, at least make sure that any blue cheeses or pungent cheeses have their own.

6. Preserve the cheeses' integrity.

I prefer not to remove the rind or otherwise trim the cheese before serving it. Even when it's not edible, the rind is part of the cheese's natural beauty. I'd rather let my guests trim it away. Nor do I cut the cheeses into individual portions unless I am serving them on individual plates, not on a platter.

accompaniments

In this book, you'll find lots of ideas for companions to cheese such as salads, compotes, nut breads, and preserved fruits. Although I often serve cheese alone, with nothing more than a fresh baguette, I do think an unexpected accompaniment can make the cheese course more inviting. Even a naturally beautiful woman puts on makeup and earrings sometimes.

My preference is for simple, seasonal accompaniments that flatter the cheeses in flavor or texture. Here are a few possibilities.

BREADS: A rustic country loaf, a baguette, or a basket of chewy dinner rolls is always appropriate. These are the most versatile bread choices as every cheese goes with them. A chewy whole-grain bread also flatters most cheeses, as long as the bread isn't sweet. Savory walnut bread is appealing with goat cheeses, triple crèmes, and blue cheeses. A dried-fruit bread with no added sugar, such as the golden raisin bread on page 26, can complement ricotta or fromage blanc, goat cheese, Munster, and triple crèmes.

I steer clear of herb bread, jalapeño bread and the like, but olive bread has some appeal with goat cheese or feta—especially at a picnic lunch or outdoor meal.

With the artisan bread movement growing as fast as the interest in cheese, most cheese lovers should have access to some good, crusty loaves. These are a better choice than crackers for the cheese board.

FRUIT: Fresh seasonal fruit is a classic cheese accompaniment. Parmigiano-Reggiano or pecorino toscano with pears; farmhouse Cheddar with apples; blue cheese with ripe figs; fresh ricotta with berries or apricots; any cheese with grapes—these are time-honored pairings that always please. Contemporary chefs and my own experimentation have suggested some new combinations—new to me, at least—that also seem utterly right: a blood orange salad with Spanish cheeses (page 99), persimmon in a green salad with the Spanish blue cheese, Cabrales (page 102), or watermelon with arugula and feta (page 79).

Shop at farmers' markets to find fruit grown locally and picked ripe. Delicious fruit that you have taken pains to obtain will make your cheese course memorable. In fall, you might offer a basket of heirloom apples with Cheddar, Dry Jack, Teleme, or Brie. In summer, serve a platter of plump halved figs with Montbriac, Fourme d'Ambert, or Crescenza.

Consider cooked fruits, too. I love roasted pears with Gorgonzola (page 42) or cranberries and pears made into a chutney for Vermont Cheddar (page 51). On the French side of the Pyrenees, people pair the local sheep's cheese with exquisite cherry preserves.

Don't forget dried fruit—served uncooked, poached in a compote, or soaked in brandy. You won't believe how tasty dried cherries are when they are plumped in kirsch and served with Alsatian Munster (page 44). Dried figs plumped in sweet sherry are the perfect match for goat Gouda (page 69), Parmigiano-Reggiano, or Manchego.

One caution: The natural sweetness and acidity in most fruit can interfere with the appreciation of wine. If you want to showcase an important old bottle with your cheese course, I probably wouldn't offer fruit at that time.

GREEN SALADS: Leafy salads to accompany cheeses might include fruit or nuts, but the salads should be simple so the cheese shines. I often use a nut oil, such as walnut or hazelnut oil, on these salads to complement the cheese.

NUTS: Serve them fresh in the shell in the fall, or shelled and toasted. Pair toasted almonds with Manchego, Majorero, or Dry Jack; toasted walnuts with goat cheese or Cheddar; toasted hazelnuts with Gruyère or Taleggio.

OLIVES: When you serve cheese before a meal, olives are a nice complement. For a simple antipasto, assemble a platter of sliced Idiazábal or pecorino pepato, sliced salami, and olives. You will find vastly better olives at a specialty store than on a supermarket shelf, and you can taste them first.

beverage choices for cheese

"Man has yet to find a better companion to cheese than wine."
—Pierre Androuet

At my house, wine and cheese are virtually inseparable at the table. In fact, their rapport means I have to finish them at the same time. If I have a little wine in my glass but no cheese left on my plate, I'll reach for more cheese. If I still have cheese on my plate but no wine in my glass, I'll pour myself another glass. This can go on for a while.

As I've broadened my knowledge of cheese, I've expanded my notion of what beverages to serve with it. In particular, I've found that Spanish sherries, both dry and sweet, are lovely companions for many cheeses. I've also enjoyed sparkling wine with triple crèmes, the recommendation of cheese authority Steven Jenkins. And I've come to realize that some exceptionally pungent cheeses may not be wine-friendly at all but are perfect with a craft beer or even a glass of fruit brandy.

Here are some guidelines for pairing wine and cheese, with the proviso that your own taste should always prevail.

In general, serve light, fresh wines with mild, fresh cheeses. Stronger cheeses can take stronger wines.

Consider the cheese's origin when choosing a wine. If only on an emotional level, cheeses often taste best with wine from their region, such as pecorino toscano with Chianti, Epoisses with Burgundy, or Vella Dry Jack with Sonoma County Zinfandel.

The cheeses that I find require the most caution in wine matching are blue cheeses. The mold in their veins, which gives them their character, can make a red wine taste metallic to me. To my surprise, a noted wine-with-food lecturer tells me that many others do not have this reaction—indeed, they like red wine with blue cheese. If you share my opinion, check the recommendations below for alternative beverages.

Clearly, if you are serving several cheeses together, a single wine will rarely complement all of them. Nevertheless, keep things simple and serve only one wine. In my experience, a medium-bodied Pinot Noir or Cabernet Sauvignon is a good all-purpose choice.

FRESH CHEESES, *such as cottage cheese, ricotta, ricotta salata, feta, and young goat cheese:* crisp white wine such as Sauvignon Blanc or French Sancerre; dry Chenin Blanc or Vouvray; young Chablis; dry rosé; young, fruity red wine such as Beaujolais, Chinon, or Bourgueil.

MORE MATURE GOAT CHEESES: Vouvray (dry or slightly off-dry); Sauvignon Blanc or French Sancerre; medium-bodied red wines from the Rhone or Provence; medium-bodied Zinfandel.

SOFT BLOOMY-RIND CHEESES, *such as Brie and Camembert:* fine red wine such as mature Bordeaux or Cabernet Sauvignon; medium-bodied Pinot Noir or Burgundy.

SOFT WASHED-RIND CHEESES, *such as Epoisses, Pont-l'Evêque, and Taleggio:* sturdy red wines such as Syrah, Barolo, Barbaresco, weightier Pinot Noirs or Burgundies.

TRIPLE-CRÈME CHEESES, *such as Brillat-Savarin, Explorateur, and Saint-André:* medium-bodied Pinot Noir or Burgundy; sparkling wine.

SEMI-FIRM TO FIRM, PRESSED-CURD CHEESES, *such as Appenzeller, Cheddar, Fontina Val d'Aosta, Gouda, Gruyère, Emmental, and Manchego:* young Cabernet Sauvignon or Bordeaux; fruity Zinfandel; Merlot; dry, nutty sherry (with Cheddar); dry Riesling (with Appenzeller, Emmental, Gruyère); Italian Nebbiolo (with Fontina Val d'Aosta).

EXCEPTIONALLY PUNGENT CHEESES, *such as Munster and Livarot:* Alsatian Gewürztraminer; full-flavored beer or fruit brandy; fino or manzanilla sherry.

BLUE CHEESES, *such as Roquefort, Gorgonzola, Cabrales, Fourme d'Ambert, and Stilton:* Sauternes or other dessert wines; Port; Spanish oloroso sherry. (To my palate, the milder blues—such as Fourme d'Ambert, Stilton, and Shropshire Blue—don't always demolish a red wine. A full-bodied red wine can stand up to them, although I prefer a sweet wine.)

MODERATELY AGED SHEEP'S-MILK CHEESES, such as Ossau-Iraty, pecorino toscano, Bellwether Farms' pecorino pepato, and Manchego: hearty and rustic red wines such as Zinfandel, Cahors, Madiran, or Chianti, or wines from Provence or the Languedoc; Spanish fino or amontillado sherry.

WELL-AGED CHEESES, such as aged Gouda, aged goat Gouda, Dry Jack, Fiore Sardo, and Parmigiano-Reggiano: mature and elegant wines from Bordeaux, Rioja, Chianti Classico, or Piedmont; mature California Cabernet Sauvignon.

storing cheese

If your seek-and-destroy refrigerator missions regularly turn up moldy or dried-out cheese, you may want to improve your handling techniques. All cheeses are perishable, but careful storage can prolong their life.

Most cheeses prefer a humid, cool environment. The dry, circulating air of a refrigerator dries them out. On the other hand, most cheeses need to "breathe"—to release their own moisture. They deteriorate if the moisture they release is trapped.

Most experts recommend a storage approach that tries to balance these two concerns—keeping the storage environment humid, yet allowing the cheese to breathe. Complicating the issue is many people's belief—one I share—that aluminum foil and some plastic wraps impart an unpleasant taste.

Nevertheless, it's no crime to simply leave many of the firmer cheeses tightly wrapped in plastic, changing the plastic every couple of days so that moisture can escape. If you find that you can taste the plastic, try another brand of wrap. If you still notice a plastic taste, or if you are dealing with moist and sticky cheeses such as Teleme or Reblochon, you will want to try some version of the following method.

Wrap the cheese in wax paper, parchment paper, or butcher paper, then overwrap with plastic. Store in your refrigerator's produce bin, which has higher humidity than the designated cheese bin in refrigerator doors. Alternatively, refrigerate the wrapped cheese in a cardboard box or in a plastic container with the lid slightly ajar.

You can store different cheeses together, although it's a good idea to keep really stinky cheeses and blue cheeses separate. The mold from blue cheese can "travel."

Even the fussiest storage system is no substitute for frequent monitoring, however. Merchants suggest that you check your cheeses often to see if they are drying out or look too moist; then you can adjust their conditions accordingly.

If you will be serving your cheeses within a day or two and your home is cool, you don't need to refrigerate them at all, except for fresh cheese such as ricotta (see below). Keep them in a cool place, wrapped, until you are ready to serve them. Their texture will be better than if they were refrigerated and then brought to room temperature, especially with soft-ripened cheeses such as Brie or Camembert.

special storage cases

FRESH CHEESE: Keep fresh cheeses, such as cottage cheese, fromage blanc, and ricotta, tightly covered and well chilled. Always bring these cheeses straight home from the store, refrigerate, and use quickly. They are highly perishable.

MOZZARELLA: At the store, fresh mozzarella should be covered in whey to keep it from drying out. (The whey is the liquid part of milk that remains after the solids are coagulated for cheese.) Ask your merchant to cover your purchase with whey; at home, keep it well chilled and use quickly.

FETA: If possible, ask your merchant to cover the feta with the brine it came in. The brine will preserve it for several days. If you purchase cut-and-wrapped feta without brine, you should use the feta within two to three days; for longer keeping, make a brine at home by dissolving salt in water in the ratio of 1 teaspoon salt per 1 cup water.

PARMIGIANO-REGGIANO, PECORINO ROMANO, AND OTHER HARD GRATING CHEESES: These cheeses have little moisture and do not need to breathe. Wrap them in wax paper, parchment paper, or butcher paper, then overwrap tightly with aluminum foil.

cheese etiquette

Because a cheese platter is typically shared, I'd like to raise an issue that makes sharing more pleasant: how to cut cheese properly when it's presented to you. I don't know of any rules on the subject, but I do think that common sense suggests a few guidelines.

The basic idea is, when possible, to cut the cheese in a way that preserves its shape for the next person and in such a way that the rind is shared. If you're the first person to cut from a wedge of Brie, for example, you should cut a thin wedge rather than cutting across the "nose." With some cheese shapes, there's no easy way to share the rind. Someone will get a disproportionately large share, but as one cheese merchant said to me, "That is perhaps a good metaphor for life."

If you're the host, try to present the cheeses so that they are easy for guests to cut. This may mean setting a wedge on its side so it's stable, or cutting a large wedge with a hard rind in half horizontally and putting the largest cut side up. Don't obsess about this, but do take a minute to think about whether it will be apparent to guests how to handle a cheese. You might even want to make the first cut as a guide.

Do you eat the rind or not? The decision is yours; there is no "right" answer. If you find the rind palatable, eat it. If it's hard or unpleasant, trim it away.

cow's-milk cheeses

Perhaps because most Americans are raised on cow's milk, many find cow's-milk cheeses the easiest to like. The range of styles is vast, from the pure milky taste of a day-old ricotta to the complex, nutty, orange-peel character of a two-year-old Parmigiano-Reggiano; from mild-mannered Teleme to an Alsatian Munster so pungent that its aroma won't stay in one room.

To help you explore these cheeses, I have arranged them in this chapter on a rough continuum from soft and fresh to aged and hard. In between, you will find creamy cheeses, blue cheeses, and firm cheeses. Don't feel bound by the complements that I have suggested for each cheese; play around with different combinations.

For example, the Prunes in Red Wine (page 23) that I have paired with Explorateur would be equally appealing with Montbriac, Gorgonzola, Gorgonzola Mascarpone Torta (page 38), Crescenza, or with any triple-crème cheese. Serve the Italian Salad and Hazelnuts (page 37) not just with Taleggio, but also with Gruyère, Cantal, or Fontina Val d'Aosta. The Mesclun and Red Pear Salad (page 32) would flatter just about any cheese in this book.

If you can't find the cheese I have specified, a good merchant can guide you to a suitable replacement.

Artisan cheesemakers in some communities are producing excellent cow's and sheep's ricottas with a light, creamy texture and the pure taste of sweet milk. They are so fresh that they deserve to be the focus of a cheese course. Packaged supermarket ricotta pales in comparison.

I like to serve ricotta after the main course with honey or sugar and seasonal fruit—peaches, berries, or figs in summer; apples and pears in fall; apricots and cherries in spring. When chestnuts show up in late fall, try poaching them in syrup and crumbling them over a mound of ricotta. Surround with sliced red pears and open a bottle of Italian vin santo or other dessert wine.

Chestnuts can be frustrating and tedious to peel. The thin inner skin wants to stick to the nut, even after blanching. You will have an easier time if you keep them in the hot blanching water until you are ready to peel them. For best flavor, poach them in the vanilla bean syrup a day ahead.

8 large fresh chestnuts

½ cup sugar

One 1-inch piece vanilla bean, halved lengthwise to expose seeds

1½ cups water

1 pound fresh whole-milk ricotta

¼ cup chestnut honey or other full-flavored honey

1 large red-skinned pear

Cut an X in the flat side of each chestnut. Bring a small pot of water to a boil over high heat. Add the chestnuts and boil for 5 minutes. Remove from the heat. Remove the chestnuts from the hot water one at a time with a slotted spoon and peel, working back from the X. If necessary, protect your hands by holding the hot chestnut in a kitchen towel. Remove both the hard outer shell and the papery brown skin, which tends to cling to the nut.

In a small saucepan, combine the sugar, vanilla bean, and water. Bring to a simmer over medium heat, stirring to dissolve the sugar. Add the chestnuts, cover, and adjust the heat to maintain a gentle simmer. Cook for 45 minutes. Let the chestnuts cool in the pan, then refrigerate overnight.

To serve, place the ricotta on a large serving platter or divide evenly among 4 dessert plates. Remove the chestnuts from the syrup and crumble them coarsely by hand. Sprinkle the chestnuts over the ricotta, then drizzle the chestnuts and ricotta with the honey. Cut the pear into thin slices and arrange alongside.

Serves 4

From Edward Behr, author of *The Art of Eating* newsletter, comes the idea of plumping prunes overnight in red wine to make an accompaniment for cheese. The prunes puff up like tiny balloons, ready to release their winy contents at the first bite. Behr recommends them, very lightly sweetened, with Roquefort. I like them a little sweeter yet, with buttery triple-crème cheeses such as Explorateur, Saint-André, or, best of all, the unctuous but hard-to-find Jean Grogne. Another incredible match for these prunes: a layered Gorgonzola Mascarpone Torta, either homemade (page 38) or store-bought (see Resources, page 104).

Put the prunes in a small bowl and add red wine to cover. Cover with a plate and let stand overnight.

Drain and measure the red wine. Put the wine in a saucepan with the sugar and simmer over medium heat until the wine is reduced by half. Pour over the prunes and let cool, then refrigerate.

Serve the cheese from a platter and pass the prunes in a bowl, or serve each diner 4 prunes and a 2-ounce portion of Explorateur.

Serves 6

24 large unpitted prunes

1½ cups dry red wine, or enough to cover prunes

3 tablespoons sugar

¾ pound Explorateur

marinated bocconcini

Italians serve *bocconcini*—literally, "little mouthfuls"—as an appetizer or part of an antipasto platter. These miniature balls of mozzarella also make perfect picnic food. Marinate them in olive oil with garlic and herbs, then surround with halved red and gold cherry tomatoes, black olives, and good bread. Save this dish for summer when markets offer flavorful, vine-ripened tomatoes; alternatively, omit the tomatoes and olives and serve the marinated bocconcini with toothpicks to accompany cocktails or apéritifs.

In a small saucepan, heat the olive oil, garlic, oregano, and pepper flakes over medium heat until the garlic sizzles and just begins to color, 1 to 2 minutes. Remove from the heat and cool to room temperature. Put the bocconcini in a bowl and cover with the seasoned oil. Add the capers and parsley. Stir to coat. Cover and let stand for several hours, stirring occasionally. Just before serving, season to taste with salt.

Arrange the bocconcini on a serving platter. Surround with the tomatoes and olives. Spoon some of the marinade over the tomatoes.

Serves 6 to 8

½ cup extra-virgin olive oil

1 large clove garlic, minced

2 teaspoons chopped fresh oregano

¼ teaspoon red pepper flakes

1 pound bocconcini, well drained

1 tablespoon capers, coarsely chopped

2 tablespoons chopped fresh parsley

Kosher or sea salt

Halved cherry tomatoes or sliced tomatoes, preferably mixed colors, for garnish

Black olives, such as Gaeta or Kalamata, for garnish

Liam Callahan at Bellwether Farms in Petaluma, California, learned to make Crescenza from cheesemakers near Milan, where a similar cheese by the same name has been made for centuries. (It's also called Stracchino in Italy.) At Bellwether Farms, the Callahans make this cow's-milk cheese in individual barrels rather than vats because the curd is so delicate. In three to four days, it is ready for sale, but its buttery flavor doesn't really develop until it is about two weeks old, says Cindy Callahan, Liam's mother and the farm's founder. At four weeks, the cheese is so runny that it has to be kept on a plate.

Crescenza has a pronounced yeasty flavor and an unctuous, creamy texture. I think it is the perfect breakfast cheese, especially on raisin toast. This recipe was adapted from the raisin bread in Carol Field's *The Italian Baker*.

2 cups golden raisins

2 cups warm water

1 tablespoon sugar

1 tablespoon active dry yeast

3¾ cups plus 3 tablespoons unbleached all-purpose flour

1½ teaspoons salt

2 teaspoons unsalted butter, at room temperature

Coarse cornmeal or polenta for dusting

1 pound Bellwether Farms' Crescenza or other soft, creamy breakfast cheese

Alternative cheeses: Fresh Robiola, Asiago fresco, Teleme, fresh goat cheese, or Tuscan pecorino fresco

Put the raisins in a small bowl and add the water. Let stand for 1 hour to soften, then drain in a sieve, reserving the raisin water. Measure the raisin water and add additional water if necessary to make 1⅓ cups.

In a small saucepan, heat raisin water gently until warm (about 110°F). Transfer to a large bowl and stir in the sugar. Sprinkle the yeast over the water and let stand until softened, 2 minutes. Whisk with a fork to dissolve the yeast and let stand for 10 minutes.

Stir together the 3¾ cups flour and salt. Add the butter to the yeast mixture, then begin adding the flour 1 cup at a time. When the mixture becomes too stiff to stir, turn out onto a floured work surface and knead until the dough is firm, smooth, and elastic, about 5 minutes, working in as much additional flour as needed.

Shape the dough into a ball and transfer to an oiled bowl. Turn to coat the dough with oil, then cover with plastic wrap and let rise until doubled, 1½ to 2 hours. »

Without punching the dough down, transfer it to a floured work surface and pat it firmly into a 14-inch circle.

Pat the raisins dry, then toss with the 3 tablespoons flour.

Sprinkle the dough surface evenly with one-third of the raisins. Fold opposite "sides" of the circle toward the center, then roll the dough into a cylinder. Again, flatten the dough as much as you can and sprinkle the surface with half of the remaining raisins, then fold in the sides and roll as before. Cover with a kitchen towel and let rest 15 minutes. Flatten the dough a third time and top with the remaining raisins, spreading them evenly. Fold in the sides and roll as before. Cut the dough in half and shape each half into a tapered loaf about 12 inches long. Try to keep the raisins tucked inside the dough as any exposed raisins will burn.

Line a baking sheet or work surface with two pieces of parchment paper. Put a loaf on each piece, cover with a kitchen towel and let rise until almost doubled, about 1 hour.

Put a baking sheet or pizza stone in the oven and preheat to 400°F for 30 minutes. Just before baking, dust the stone with cornmeal. Carefully pick up a loaf from underneath the parchment paper. Gently invert the loaf, remove the paper, then invert the loaf again onto the hot stone. Repeat with second loaf. Bake for 5 minutes, then lower the oven temperature to 375°F and continue baking until the bread is well browned and firm, about 30 minutes. Transfer to a rack to cool completely before slicing.

Save one of the loaves for the next day or freeze for longer keeping. Slice the other loaf and toast on both sides. Serve the hot toast with Crescenza.

Serves 8

baked ricotta with parsley salad

Beaten with egg and baked in a pie tin, ricotta puffs up into a stunning, golden brown dome. It does deflate as it cools, but then you can slice the barely warm cheese like a pie. Serve it with a green salad or, as here, with a parsley and tomato salad. For best flavor, use the intensely sweet, small cherry tomatoes—such as Sweet 100s and Sungolds—found at farmers' markets in summer. You can eat the parsley salad immediately, but I like it better when it has rested for about an hour to "fatigue" the parsley. Add some crusty bread and white wine and call it a lunch.

Note that the ricotta needs to drain for several hours or overnight before baking.

To make the baked ricotta: Put the ricotta in a large sieve or colander lined with a double thickness of cheesecloth. Cover the ricotta with the cheesecloth, set the sieve or colander over a bowl to catch the draining whey, and set a plate with a weight (such as a heavy can of tomatoes) on top of the ricotta to speed draining. Refrigerate for several hours or overnight.

Preheat the oven to 375°F. Butter a 10-inch pie pan. In a large bowl, stir together the ricotta and Parmigiano-Reggiano. Season to taste with salt and pepper. Stir in the eggs, beating well. Transfer the mixture to the prepared pan, spreading it evenly. Bake in the upper third of the oven until puffed and lightly brown, about 55 minutes. Let cool, then unmold onto a cutting board.

To make the parsley salad: In a large bowl, combine all the ingredients. Toss well. Taste and adjust the seasonings. Serve immediately or let stand for up to 1 hour, tossing occasionally.

Cut the ricotta into 8 wedges and place on individual plates. Accompany each serving with some of the parsley salad.

Serves 8

BAKED RICOTTA

2 pounds or two 15-ounce containers whole-milk ricotta

⅓ cup freshly grated Parmigiano-Reggiano

Salt and freshly ground black pepper

2 eggs

PARSLEY SALAD

6 cups loosely packed Italian parsley leaves, stems removed (about 1½ bunches)

½ pint red cherry tomatoes, halved

½ pint golden cherry tomatoes, halved

½ small red onion, cut into paper-thin slices

1 small clove garlic, minced

2½ tablespoons extra-virgin olive oil

2 to 3 teaspoons red wine vinegar, or more as needed

Salt and freshly ground black pepper

Made by the Peluso family since the 1920s, Teleme is uniquely Californian. Frank Peluso, who runs Peluso Cheese now, says his Italian father was initially trying to make Stracchino, the soft-ripened Italian cheese, but missed the mark slightly. Like Stracchino, Teleme becomes runnier and more flavorful as it ages. At two weeks, it is pale and mild, bulging slightly in its rice flour–covered rind. By four weeks, it has developed more tang and is hard to contain when sliced.

I particularly like it as a picnic cheese with crusty bread and summer fruits, such as apricots, cherries, and peaches. But with the growing popularity of truffle oil, I have also discovered the appeal of ripe Teleme drizzled with a few drops of this pungent condiment. Serve with homemade flatbread and a Pinot Noir, California Sangiovese, or Italian Chianti. Note that you need to start the flatbread one day ahead.

SPONGE

1 cup warm water

1 teaspoon active dry yeast

1 cup unbleached all-purpose flour

DOUGH

1/2 cup water

1/3 cup dry white wine

1/3 cup extra-virgin olive oil

1 tablespoon kosher salt

2 tablespoons cornmeal

2 3/4 cups unbleached all-purpose
    flour

2 tablespoons plus 2 teaspoons
    extra-virgin olive oil

1 teaspoon coarse salt

1 pound Teleme cheese

White or black truffle oil

To make the sponge: One day ahead, put the warm water in a medium bowl. Sprinkle the yeast over the surface and let stand for 2 minutes, then whisk with a fork until dissolved. Add the flour and stir with a wooden spoon until smooth. Cover and let stand at room temperature for 24 hours.

To make the dough: Put the sponge in a heavy-duty mixer with a paddle attachment. Add the water, wine, olive oil, salt, and cornmeal and mix on low speed. Gradually add the flour to make a soft dough. The dough will hold together but will be moist and a little sticky. Knead in the mixer for 5 minutes with the paddle attachment. Scrape down the sides and the paddle, cover the bowl with plastic wrap, and let the dough rise for 1½ hours, or until doubled.

Generously grease a 12-by-17-inch heavy-rimmed baking sheet with the 2 teaspoons olive oil. Transfer the dough to the baking sheet and, with oiled fingers, pat and prod it into place. It will be too elastic to cover the sheet completely and it will want to bounce back; let dough rest for 5 minutes, then pat again. If it still refuses to cover the sheet completely, let dough rest again for 5 to 10 minutes, then pat again. Let rise until puffy, about 1½ hours.

While dough rises, position a rack in the center of the oven. Line the oven rack with baking tiles or a baking stone. Preheat the oven to 550°F or the highest setting for at least 45 minutes.

Brush the surface of the dough with the 2 tablespoons olive oil, then dimple the dough vigorously with your fingertips. Sprinkle with the coarse salt. Bake until browned and firm, about 15 minutes. Slide onto a rack to cool.

At serving time, place the cheese on a platter and drizzle very lightly with truffle oil. (Don't overdo it; truffle oil is pungent.) Cut the flatbread into 1-inch-wide fingers or another desired shape and pass with the cheese.

Serves 8

mesclun and red pear salad with triple-crème tartines

Unctuous triple-crème cheeses satisfy in small portions. They are extremely high in butterfat (75 percent by weight or more), which explains their luxurious texture. One of the best ways to enjoy these over-the-top cheeses is to spread a little on toast and serve with a salad, which balances their richness. In France a tartine is, typically, a piece of rustic bread or baguette topped with a sweet or savory spread—in this case, with buttery cheese.

Be sure to buy your pear in time to allow it to ripen. Leave it at room temperature until it gives slightly at the stem end.

VINAIGRETTE

3 tablespoons extra-virgin olive oil

1 tablespoon red wine vinegar

1 shallot, minced

Salt and freshly ground black pepper

8 slices country-style bread, about 4 inches by 3 inches by ¼ inch thick, or 8 slices baguette, cut on the diagonal

⅓ pound mesclun

1 large red-skinned pear

¼ pound Explorateur, Saint-André, Brillat-Savarin, or other triple-crème cheese

To make the vinaigrette: In a small bowl, whisk together the oil, vinegar, shallot, and salt and pepper to taste. Let stand 30 minutes to allow shallot flavor to mellow. Taste and adjust the balance as needed.

Preheat a broiler or toaster oven. Toast the bread on both sides. In a large bowl, toss the mesclun with enough of the dressing to coat the leaves lightly; you may not need it all. Taste and adjust the seasoning.

Divide the greens among four plates. Cut the pear into thin slices and nestle among the greens. Spread the cheese on toasts and place alongside the greens.

Serves 4

Montbriac is a French cow's-milk cheese with a thin dark rind and a buttery, Brie-like interior lightly ribboned with blue veins. At Bistro Jeanty in California's Napa Valley, chef Philippe Jeanty serves it with a dried-fruit compote—a splendid idea that I've borrowed, although the compote below is my own.

Please make an effort to find plump, moist, high-quality dried fruit, which you are more likely to see at a farmers' market than at a supermarket. With mediocre dried fruit, this compote seems uninspired. The Dean & DeLuca market in St. Helena, California, sells a one-pound package of mixed California dried fruit that is superb (see Resources, page 104). You can use any dried fruit totaling about one pound, but try to make a pretty assortment of colors and shapes.

In a stainless steel saucepan, combine the wine, water, sugar, cinnamon, clove, vanilla, and bay leaf. Bring to a simmer over medium heat, stirring to dissolve the sugar.

Poach each type of fruit separately as cooking times differ. Poach, covered, in the barely simmering syrup until the fruit is plump and tender but not mushy, then remove with a slotted spoon to a serving dish. Although cooking time will vary depending on the size and dryness of the fruit, pears, plums, and cherries take about 15 minutes, raisins as little as 3 minutes. Remove the cinnamon, clove, vanilla, and bay leaf after poaching the pears or the flavor will get too strong.

Let the syrup cool, then stir in the brandy. Taste and add a squeeze of lemon, if needed, to brighten the flavor. If the syrup seems too thick or intense, thin with water. Pour over the fruit.

To serve, divide the cheese among 6 plates. Lift the fruit out of the syrup with a slotted spoon and divide among the plates.

Serves 6

2 cups white wine

1 cup water

⅞ cup sugar

One 2-inch piece cinnamon stick

1 clove

One 1-inch piece vanilla bean, halved lengthwise

1 bay leaf

5 ounces dried pear halves (about 6), halved lengthwise

4 ounces dried plum halves (about 12)

4 ounces dried cherries (about 30 large)

3 ounces golden raisins (scant ½ cup)

1 to 1½ tablespoons clear fruit brandy, such as pear brandy or kirsch

Lemon juice

¾ pound Montbriac

Alternative cheeses: Bleu de Bresse or Fourme d'Ambert

At Bistro Don Giovanni, a popular restaurant near my Napa Valley home, *insalata tricolore* is always on the menu. *Il tricolore* is the Italian flag—red, white, and green—but it's also a fitting name for the bistro's colorful salad of radicchio, Belgian endive, and arugula. Chef Donna Scala serves it with shavings of *grana Padano.* I omit the *grana,* add toasted hazelnuts, and serve it with Italian Taleggio, an earthy, nutty cheese with a creamy texture.

Don't settle for an underripe or overripe Taleggio; ask to taste the cheese at the store. If it's chalky (underripe) or ammoniated (overripe), leave it behind.

Serve a substantial red wine with Taleggio—a French Burgundy or California Pinot Noir, perhaps, or, to reflect the cheese's Northern Italian origins, an Italian Barbaresco or Barolo.

VINAIGRETTE

3 tablespoons hazelnut or walnut oil

1 tablespoon sherry vinegar

1 shallot, minced

Salt and freshly ground black pepper

¾ cup hazelnuts

3 Belgian endives

½ small head radicchio

3 ounces young, small arugula (about 4 cups), stems removed

¾ pound Taleggio cheese

To make the vinaigrette: In a small bowl, whisk together the oil, vinegar, shallot, and salt and pepper to taste. Let stand 30 minutes to allow shallot flavor to mellow. Taste and adjust the balance as needed.

Preheat oven to 350°F. Toast the hazelnuts on a rimmed baking sheet until fragrant and lightly colored, about 15 minutes. Immediately wrap them in a kitchen towel and rub vigorously in the towel to remove as much of the skins as possible. (Don't worry if a lot of skin adheres.) Chop the nuts coarsely.

Halve each endive lengthwise and remove the core. Cut crosswise into ½-inch pieces. Core the radicchio and tear into bite-size pieces. In a serving bowl, combine endive, radicchio, arugula, and hazelnuts. Add enough of the dressing to coat the leaves lightly; you may not need it all. Toss well, then taste and adjust the seasoning.

To serve, pass salad and cheese separately. Alternatively, divide both among 6 plates.

Serves 6

gorgonzola mascarpone torta

At the Oakville Grocery in the Napa Valley, this dramatic layered torta is the most popular choice at the cheese counter. Company employees Richard Tarlov and Joyce McCollum kindly shared the method with me. I would serve it with a sweet dessert wine.

1 pound aged Gorgonzola, well chilled

10 to 12 ounces mascarpone, well chilled

¼ cup slivered almonds

Have the cheese merchant cut the Gorgonzola horizontally with a cheese wire into 3 layers, each about 1 inch thick. You can also do this at home with a length of dental floss held taut between your hands.

Put the bottom wedge of Gorgonzola on a small tray or cutting board. Top with a ½-inch-thick layer of mascarpone, spreading it evenly. Top the mascarpone with the middle wedge of Gorgonzola. Top that wedge with another ½-inch-thick layer of mascarpone. Top the mascarpone with the remaining wedge of Gorgonzola. Frost the top and rind of the torta with ¼ inch of mascarpone. Cover the torta with an inverted crock or plastic container to protect it from the drying air of the refrigerator. Refrigerate for at least 4 hours or as long as overnight.

Preheat the oven to 325°F. Toast the almonds on a baking sheet until lightly browned, about 10 minutes. Let cool completely.

Remove the torta from the refrigerator at least 4 hours before serving and press the almonds lightly on the mascarpone-frosted top and rind. If you would like to cut the torta in half so you can put a portion on each of two cheese boards, do it while it is cold. Set the torta on its side so that the layers are face up, cover again, and let come to room temperature before serving.

Serves 12

stilton with port-glazed pears

As these poached pears rest in their Port poaching syrup, they turn a rich garnet color. I serve them halved, sliced, and fanned with some of the ruby syrup, with Stilton alongside. If you can get your hands on the superb Colston Bassett Stilton, you are in for a treat.

In a small saucepan, bring the Port, water, sugar, and lemon zest to a boil over medium heat, stirring until the sugar dissolves. While the mixture heats, peel the pears. Add the pears to the simmering liquid, setting them on their sides. Cover with a round of parchment paper that just fits over the pears, tucking it around them. Adjust the heat to maintain a gentle simmer and cook for 15 minutes.

1 cup ruby Port
1 cup water
½ cup sugar
4 strips lemon zest
2 ripe but firm pears
1½ to 2 tablespoons lemon juice
6 to 8 ounces Stilton cheese

Lift the parchment and turn the pears over in the liquid so they cook evenly. Re-cover and continue cooking until they are just tender when pierced, 10 to 12 more minutes. Remember that they will continue to cook as they cool.

Transfer the pears with a slotted spoon to a refrigerator container. Simmer the poaching liquid over medium heat until reduced to ½ cup. Let cool completely, then add the lemon juice. Pour over pears, cover, and refrigerate for at least 8 hours. Turn the pears in the syrup every couple of hours so they develop a deep burgundy color.

To serve, cut the pears in half lengthwise and core with a melon baller. Put each pear half on a cutting board, cut side down. Thinly slice lengthwise, leaving the slices attached at the stem end. Gently press on the pear to fan the slices. Put a generous tablespoon of Port syrup on each of 4 dessert plates. With a metal spatula, transfer a pear fan to each plate, placing it over the sauce. Place a slice of Stilton on each plate.

Serves 4

aged gorgonzola with honey-roasted pears

It would be hard to improve on a platter of fresh pears and honey-drizzled blue cheese, but there's always room for a variation. For roasting, you will need firm pears that are perhaps a day away from full ripeness; perfectly ripe pears will be too soft for cooking. A melon baller cores them easily, and parchment paper keeps them from browning as they cook.

Ideally, choose an aged Gorgonzola (sometimes called mountain Gorgonzola) over the mild, young Gorgonzola *dolce;* the former has a firmer texture and more developed flavor. Accompany with a Sauternes or other white dessert wine.

¼ cup white wine

2 tablespoons honey

1½ tablespoons unsalted butter, cut into small pieces

¼ teaspoon coarsely cracked black pepper

2 ripe but firm large pears

½ lemon

6 ounces aged Gorgonzola, cut into 4 pieces

Alternative cheeses: any other blue cheese

Preheat the oven to 400°F. Put the wine, honey, butter, and pepper in a shallow nonreactive baking dish, such as a glass or ceramic pie pan. Peel, halve, and core the pears. Rub with the lemon half to prevent browning. Put the pear halves, cut side down, in the baking dish. Cover with a round of parchment paper, tucking the paper loosely around the pears.

Bake until the pears are just tender when pierced, 15 to 30 minutes, depending on ripeness. Do not overcook or they will be mushy. With a metal spatula, carefully transfer pears to a platter. Pour the baking juices into a small saucepan and reduce them over high heat to ¼ cup.

Serve the pears warm, not hot. Just before serving, put each pear half on a cutting board, cut side down. Thinly slice lengthwise, leaving the slices attached at the stem end. Transfer with a metal spatula to the dessert plates. Gently press on the pear to fan the slices. Spoon 1 tablespoon of the baking juices over each pear and put a piece of Gorgonzola alongside.

Serves 4

mesclun with dried figs, blue cheese, and toasted almonds

At Citizen Cake, a popular bakery-cafe in San Francisco, the kitchen makes generous sandwiches on house-made bread and creative salads such as this one using mixed baby greens. Serve in large portions for a light lunch, or after the main course at dinner.

To make the vinaigrette: In a small bowl, whisk together the oil, vinegar, shallot, and salt and pepper to taste. Set aside for 30 minutes to allow shallot flavor to mellow. Taste and adjust the balance as needed.

Preheat the oven to 325°F. Toast the almonds on a baking sheet until lightly browned and fragrant, about 10 minutes. Let cool.

In a large bowl, combine the mesclun and figs. Add enough dressing to coat the leaves lightly; you may not need it all. Toss well. Add the cheese, breaking it into small clumps. Toss again gently. Taste and adjust the seasoning. Divide the salad among 4 plates, taking care to divide figs and cheese evenly. Top each portion with some of the almonds. Serve immediately.

Serves 4

VINAIGRETTE

¼ cup extra-virgin olive oil

1 tablespoon plus 1 teaspoon sherry vinegar

1 large shallot, minced

Salt and freshly ground black pepper

⅓ cup slivered almonds

½ pound mesclun

8 dried figs, quartered if small, in sixths if large

¼ pound blue cheese such as Stilton, Fourme d'Ambert, Roquefort, or Great Hill Blue

alsatian munster with dried cherries in kirsch

If you like pungent cheeses, the kind that infuse your car on the way home from the store, you can't help but love Alsatian Munster. It is wonderfully stinky when ripe, a heady experience for the true cheese enthusiast. Alsatians often serve it with cumin or caraway seed, perhaps to counter one pronounced flavor with another.

Alsace also produces France's most seductive *eaux de vie* (fruit brandies), so it seems natural to serve Munster with one of them, at least indirectly. Make these kirsch-soaked cherries two days ahead to allow time for them to absorb their bath. Add some chewy, bakery-made rye bread and pour an Alsatian Gewürztraminer or a top-quality kirsch.

Alsatian Munster is made in more than one size. Your merchant may carry "mini" Munsters that are about 8 ounces each, or larger rounds that range from slightly more than a pound to a pound and a half. However you purchase it, figure about two ounces per person.

---

4 dozen large dried cherries, prefer-
ably unpitted
½ cup kirsch, or as needed to cover
the cherries
About 1 pound Alsatian Munster
1 loaf rye bread, sliced

Two days before serving, put the cherries in a jar and cover with the kirsch. Let stand at room temperature for 48 hours. The cherries will absorb the kirsch and grow plump and soft.

Cut the Munster into 8 portions. Divide the cheese and cherries among 8 plates. Pass the rye bread separately.

Serves 8

Perhaps it's simply association that makes Fontina Val d'Aosta remind me of white truffles. Both the cheese and the truffles come from Piedmont, in northwest Italy, and they are sometimes paired at the table—as in *fonduta*, an Italian fondue with white truffle shaved over it.

I think a crisp, simple radicchio salad makes a perfect match for this earthy cheese. You can introduce a hint of truffle with just a few drops of truffle oil in the salad; if you choose not to, use your best extra-virgin olive oil.

Pour a medium-bodied red wine with this dish, such as an Italian Barbera, a Burgundy, or a California or Oregon Pinot Noir. The vinegar in the salad is so restrained that it won't harm the wine.

In a bowl, combine the radicchio, olive oil, and salt and pepper to taste. Toss well. Add balsamic vinegar to taste, using restraint. If desired, add a few drops of truffle oil. Be careful; it can easily be overwhelming. Add just enough to taste its presence.

Pass the salad and cheese separately, or divide the salad and cheese among 6 individual plates.

Serves 6

1 head radicchio (about 12 ounces), quartered, cored, and thinly sliced

2½ tablespoons extra-virgin olive oil

Salt and freshly ground black pepper

Balsamic vinegar

White truffle oil (optional)

¾ pound Fontina Val d'Aosta

escarole and gruyère salad with walnut oil

Enjoy this salad in winter when escarole is at its best. You will probably have to trim away a lot of dark leaves to reach the pale, crisp heart, but don't throw them away. Slice them into ribbons and add them to chicken-rice soup, or braise in olive oil with garlic and toss with pasta.

I would serve this salad after the main course and continue pouring whatever wine was on the table. I like red wine with Gruyère, but a dry Riesling would work, too.

VINAIGRETTE

1½ tablespoons olive oil

1½ tablespoons walnut oil

1½ tablespoons sherry vinegar

1 large shallot, minced

Salt and freshly ground black pepper

½ cup walnuts

2 heads escarole, pale heart only, trimmed

⅓ pound Gruyère, trimmed of any rind and cut into matchstick-size pieces

¼ cup minced Italian parsley

Alternative cheeses: Comté or Emmental

To make the vinaigrette: In a small bowl, whisk together the oils, vinegar, shallot, and salt and pepper to taste. Let stand 30 minutes to allow shallot flavor to mellow. Taste and adjust the balance as needed.

Preheat the oven to 350°F. Toast the walnuts on a baking sheet until fragrant and lightly colored, about 15 minutes. Let cool. Break any large pieces up by hand.

In a large salad bowl, combine the escarole, walnuts, Gruyère, and parsley. Add enough of the dressing to coat the salad lightly; you may not need it all. Toss well. Season with salt and pepper to taste and toss again. Serve immediately.

Serves 4 to 6

Farmers' markets and some supermarkets are beginning to offer the handsome Italian *cipolline* onions (pronounced chih-po-LEE-nay). They are as small as boiling onions but flattened, as if something sat on them. Cipolline have tan skins and mild flesh that, like all onion flesh, turns sweet when cooked. Glazing them with sherry, raisins, and honey makes these unusual onions a pleasing counterpoint to sharp cheeses. Serve them with a fine English or domestic Cheddar and a glass of Port.

1½ pounds cipolline onions

¾ cup dry sherry

⅓ cup raisins

3 tablespoons honey

3 tablespoons water

1½ tablespoons butter

1 teaspoon chopped fresh thyme

Salt and freshly ground black pepper

1 tablespoon sherry vinegar, or more to taste

½ pound English farmhouse Cheddar

Bring a large pot of water to a boil over high heat. Add the onions and boil for 2 to 3 minutes, depending on size, then drain. When cool enough to handle, slice off the root ends. Remove the outer papery onion skins; they should slip off easily.

In a 12-inch skillet, combine the onions, sherry, raisins, honey, water, butter, and thyme. Bring to a simmer over moderately high heat. Cover and adjust the heat to maintain a simmer. Cook until the onions are tender when pierced, 15 to 20 minutes. Uncover, season with salt and pepper to taste, and simmer until the sauce is reduced almost to a glaze, stirring the onions a few times so they color evenly. Remove from heat and let cool slightly in pan. Stir in the sherry vinegar.

Serve at room temperature with the farmhouse Cheddar.

Serves 6

vermont cheddar with cranberry pear chutney

The expert Cheddars made by Vermont cheesemakers—among them, Grafton Village, Shelburne Farms, and Cabot Creamery—belong on the cheese tray alongside the world's other great cheeses. But if you want to show one off, serve it alone, with a spoonful of homemade chutney.

This recipe makes about 5½ cups of chutney—more than you would need for most occasions. Leftover chutney freezes well; put some away for the Thanksgiving turkey.

This chutney, like most, is hard on wine because of the sugar and vinegar. For that reason, I would serve Cheddar with chutney on an occasion when we were drinking beer or cider already—at a picnic, perhaps, or a simple lunch. A sweet sherry might also work.

Preheat the oven to 350°F. Toast the walnuts on a baking sheet until fragrant and lightly colored, about 15 minutes. Let cool, then chop coarsely.

In a 4-quart saucepan, combine the cranberries, pears, sugar, vinegar, and ginger. Tie the cinnamon stick and clove in a piece of cheesecloth and add to saucepan. Bring to a simmer over medium heat, then adjust the heat to maintain a simmer. Cook uncovered until the cranberries have collapsed and the pears are almost tender, 15 to 20 minutes.

Stir the raisins into the chutney and cook for 5 minutes. Remove from the heat and stir in the walnuts. When cool, remove cheesecloth bag. Refrigerate in a covered container.

Divide the cheese into 8 equal portions and arrange on 8 dessert plates. Place a dollop of chutney alongside.

Serves 8

CHUTNEY

1 cup chopped walnuts

1 bag (12 ounces) cranberries

2 pounds pears, peeled, quartered, cored, and diced

2 cups sugar

1 cup cider vinegar

One 2-inch piece fresh ginger, peeled and grated

One 4-inch cinnamon stick

1 clove

¾ cup raisins

1 pound Vermont Cheddar

Alternative cheeses: English farmhouse Cheddars, Matos St. George (California), or Cantal

Apple pie and Cheddar cheese have a long association. Here's a twist on that theme—a rustic apple galette, or tart, served warm with shavings of nutty aged Gouda from Holland. Be sure to buy aged Gouda, not the undistinguished young version packaged in red paraffin and cellophane. At the other extreme, some Gouda is aged so long that it's crumbly and impossible to shave. Buy a piece you can shave with a cheese plane.

DOUGH

2 cups unbleached all-purpose flour

¾ teaspoon salt

½ cup (1 stick) cold, unsalted butter, cut into small pieces

7 tablespoons cold solid vegetable shortening, cut into small pieces

About ¼ cup ice water

1½ pounds apples

2 to 3 tablespoons granulated sugar

1 egg yolk whisked with 1 teaspoon water

About 1 tablespoon coarse sugar

¾ pound aged Gouda

Alternative cheeses: farmhouse Cheddars or Gruyère

To make the dough: In a food processor, combine the flour and salt. Pulse three or four times to blend. Add the butter and pulse a few times, just until evenly distributed and coated with flour. Add the shortening pieces and pulse a few times, just until coated with flour. There should still be pieces of flour-coated fat about the size of large peas. Transfer the mixture to a bowl. Drizzle with the ice water while tossing with a fork, just until the dough begins to come together into clumps, then gather together with your hands. You may have to knead the dough slightly to get it to hold together, but that's better than adding more water. Handling the dough as little as possible, shape it into a thick, round patty, then wrap it in plastic wrap and refrigerate until chilled, at least 2 hours.

Preheat the oven to 425°F.

Quarter, core, and peel the apples. Cut into slices about 3/16 inch thick. Set aside in a medium bowl.

Put dough on a lightly floured work surface, top with a fresh sheet of plastic wrap, and let stand 10 minutes to warm slightly. With the plastic wrap in place to keep the dough from touching the rolling pin, roll the dough into a 15-inch circle. If it threatens to stick to the work surface, slide a long knife under the dough to separate it from the surface, then reflour the work surface lightly. You may need to add a second piece of plastic wrap as the dough circle gets larger. »

Transfer the dough to a rimless baking sheet. Trim the edges as needed to make a 15-inch circle, reserving the trimmings. About 2 inches from the edge of the dough, arrange the apple slices in a neat ring, overlapping the slices slightly. Fill the center of the circle with apple slices, arranging them neatly. Sprinkle the apples with 2 to 3 tablespoons granulated sugar, depending on their sweetness.

Gently fold the edge of the dough over the apples to make a wide border, making sure there are no cracks in the dough for juices to slip through. Patch, if necessary, with bits of trimmed dough lightly moistened with cold water.

Brush the border with a little egg wash, then sprinkle the border generously with the coarse sugar. Bake until the crust is golden and the apples are tender, about 50 minutes. Slide a long knife under the galette to make sure it isn't sticking to the baking sheet, then slide onto a rack to cool slightly. Serve warm, with shavings of aged Gouda alongside each portion.

Serves 10

vella dry jack, medjool dates, and toasted walnuts

Ig Vella's Dry Jack, with its nutty, sharp, golden interior and its handsome cocoa-dusted rind, is one of California's most remarkable cheeses. It is a picnic cheese par excellence, served with fennel salami and red wine; but I also like it at the end of dinner with plump Medjool dates and lightly browned walnuts. If you have access to pale, fresh dates in autumn, do use them; they are a treat. What to drink? A hearty Zinfandel would work, but I vote for an oloroso or cream sherry from Spain.

Preheat the oven to 350°F. Toast the walnuts on a baking sheet until fragrant and lightly colored, about 15 minutes. Let cool.

Cut the cheese into ¼-inch-thick slices. Divide cheese, walnuts, and dates among 4 dessert plates.

Serves 4

24 large walnut halves

6 ounces Vella Dry Jack cheese

8 large Medjool dates, pitted and halved

Alternative cheese: Parmigiano-Reggiano or aged goat Gouda

goat's-milk cheeses

Goat cheeses figure on a long list of foods I had never tasted until I went to France during college. There, at the charming farmers' market in Aix-en-Provence, I encountered goat cheese in all its variety and glory, handmade and escorted to the market by the makers.

I remember soft, fresh, snow-white cheeses scooped from bowls; small rounds wrapped in chestnut leaves; ash-coated pyramids; and logs covered with wrinkled white mold, displayed on straw mats. The tastes were strange to me: chalky, tangy, and unlike any cheese I had tasted before. Above all, the tiny, rock-hard *crottins* puzzled me. Why would anyone want to eat something so dry and ugly?

Slowly, over six months in France, I grew to like that tangy taste of young goat cheese and to appreciate the character that develops with age. Today, I relish goat cheeses at every stage and revel in our many choices. I don't have to dream of a trip back to Aix-en-Provence (although, admittedly, I do) to find a superb goat cheese selection.

Markets today carry many domestic goat cheeses, such as the ash-enhanced Humboldt Fog from California's Cypress Grove Chèvre, the exquisite Taupinière from California's Laura Chenel, or the Pepper Brick from Coach Farms in New York. Add to that the vastly expanded array of imported goat cheeses—such as Spanish Garrotxa, Dutch goat Gouda, and French Cabécou—and it's easy to feel rich with options.

In this chapter, I also tell you how to make two fresh goat cheeses in your own kitchen, a simple and satisfying activity that may—who knows?—lure you into a new hobby.

lebanese yogurt cheese with za'atar and olives

A typical Lebanese breakfast includes a plate of thick, homemade yogurt cheese *(lubneh)* topped with olive oil and herbs and served with olives and bread. I suspect most Americans would prefer that combination at dinner, where it makes an appealing beginning to a Mediterranean meal. I would add radishes to the platter; for a more substantial hors d'oeuvre, you could add cucumbers, cooked beets, and green onions.

Za'atar, a Middle Eastern herb blend frequently sprinkled on lubneh, varies from maker to maker, but a typical mixture includes thyme, sumac, sesame seeds, and oregano. You can purchase za'atar from the Spice House (see Resources, page 104).

Line a sieve with cheesecloth. If the cheesecloth is loosely woven (most supermarket brands are), use a triple thickness. Pour the yogurt into the sieve, then gather the edges of the cheesecloth and tie into a bag. Hang the bag over the sink or over a bowl to catch the drippings. Let drain for 8 hours.

Turn the soft, creamy cheese out onto a platter. Season the surface with salt to taste, drizzle with olive oil, then sprinkle generously with za'atar. Surround the cheese with the olives and radishes. Serve with the warm pita bread wedges.

1 quart goat's-milk yogurt

Kosher or sea salt

2 tablespoons extra-virgin olive oil

Za'atar herb blend

24 Kalamata olives

1 bunch small radishes, trimmed

Pita bread, cut into wedges, warmed

Serves 6

grape focaccia with homemade goat fromage blanc

With a purchased starter culture and storebought goat's milk, you can make homemade fromage blanc in less than a day. Enjoy it with sugared grape focaccia for dessert, or season it with minced shallots and herbs and serve it for lunch with radishes, cucumbers, and pita bread. Note that you will also need an instant-read thermometer and cheesecloth. Alternatively, serve the focaccia with store-bought fromage blanc or ricotta.

FOCACCIA SPONGE

1 cup warm water (about 110°F)

1 teaspoon active dry yeast

1 cup unbleached all-purpose flour

GOAT FROMAGE BLANC

2 quarts goat's milk

1 package fromage blanc direct-set
   culture (see Resources, page 104)

Salt

FOCACCIA DOUGH

½ cup water

⅓ cup dry white wine

⅓ cup olive oil

1½ teaspoons kosher salt

2 tablespoons cornmeal

2¾ cups unbleached all-purpose
   flour

2 tablespoons plus 2 teaspoons
   extra-virgin olive oil

½ pound seedless red grapes, halved

¼ cup coarse sugar or granulated
   sugar

To make the focaccia sponge: One day ahead, put the warm water in a medium bowl. Sprinkle the yeast over the surface and let stand 2 minutes, then whisk with a fork until dissolved. Add the flour and stir with a wooden spoon until smooth. Cover and let stand at room temperature for 24 hours.

To make the goat fromage blanc: In a medium saucepan, heat the milk over medium heat to 170°F on an instant-read thermometer, stirring occasionally. Immediately transfer the saucepan to an ice bath to cool the milk quickly to 72°F. Remove the saucepan from the ice bath and stir in the fromage blanc culture. Cover and let stand at room temperature, preferably at 72°F, until mixture sets into a solid, yogurtlike custard, 12 to 15 hours or more. Line a colander with a double thickness of cheesecloth. Gently ladle the curd into the cheesecloth, then lift the edges of the cloth to form a bag. Tie the bag shut and suspend over the sink or over a bowl to drain until the fromage blanc is as thick as you like, 4 to 6 hours. You may need to open the bag once and scrape some of the thickened cheese away from the surface of the cheesecloth to speed draining. Transfer to a bowl and stir in salt to taste.

To make the focaccia dough: Put the sponge in a heavy-duty mixer with a paddle attachment. Add the water, wine, olive oil, salt, and cornmeal and mix on low speed. With the mixer running, gradually add the flour to make a soft dough. The dough

»

will hold together but will be moist and a little sticky. Knead in the mixer for 5 minutes with the paddle attachment. Scrape down the sides and the paddle, cover the bowl with plastic wrap, and let the dough rise 1½ hours.

Generously grease a 12-by-17-inch rimmed baking sheet with the 2 teaspoons olive oil. Transfer the dough to the baking sheet and, with oiled fingers, pat and stretch it to cover the sheet. It will be too elastic to cover the sheet completely and it will want to bounce back; let the dough rest for 5 minutes, then stretch again. If it still refuses to cover the sheet completely, let the dough rest again for 5 to 10 minutes, then stretch again. Let rise until puffy, about 1½ hours. (Do not cover the dough; it is so moist that a towel will stick to it.)

While the dough rises, position a rack in the center of the oven. Line the rack with baking tiles or a baking stone. Preheat the oven to 550°F or the highest setting for at least 45 minutes.

Brush the surface of the dough with the 2 tablespoons olive oil. Top with the grapes, cut side down, pressing them gently into the dough. Sprinkle the surface evenly with sugar, then dimple the dough vigorously with your fingertips. Bake until browned and firm, about 15 minutes. Carefully remove the focaccia from the pan and slide onto a rack to cool.

Slice the focaccia into thick fingers. Serve each diner several pieces with a dollop of fromage blanc on the side.

Makes one 12-by-17-inch focaccia

baby greens with roasted beets and warm goat cheese toasts

A young, firm goat cheese turns soft and creamy when warmed briefly in the oven. Spread the softened cheese on crisp toast and serve with a salad—here, a green salad with wedges of roasted beets. This dish would be a first course in my house, served with a California Sauvignon Blanc or French Pouilly-Fumé. On another occasion, serve the goat cheese toasts on their own to accompany apéritifs.

If you buy beets with greens attached, save the beet greens for a cooked salad the following day.

Preheat the oven to 400°F. Remove the beet greens, if attached, leaving 1 inch of stem to avoid piercing the skin. Put the beets in a baking dish (use separate dishes for red and golden beets as red beets "bleed"). Add ¼ inch of water, cover, and bake until the beets are tender when pierced, 40 minutes to 1 hour, depending on size. Add more water if the beets threaten to cook dry. When the beets are cool enough to handle, peel and cut into wedges.

In a small bowl, whisk together 2 tablespoons of the olive oil, 1 tablespoon of the walnut oil, the sherry vinegar, the shallot, and salt and pepper to taste. Let stand for 30 minutes to allow the shallot flavor to mellow. Taste and adjust the seasoning.

Preheat the broiler. With a serrated knife, slice the baguette on a sharp diagonal to make 4 dramatic slices about 7 inches long and ¼ inch thick. (You will have leftover bread.) Using 1 tablespoon of the olive oil, brush the slices lightly on both sides. Put on a baking sheet and broil on both sides until lightly browned.

Reduce oven temperature to 350°F. Put the goat cheese in a lightly oiled baking dish and top with the 1 teaspoon olive oil.

8 small or 4 medium beets, preferably an assortment of golden beets and red beets

3 tablespoons plus 1 teaspoon extra-virgin olive oil

1 tablespoon walnut oil

1 tablespoon sherry vinegar

1 shallot, minced

Salt and freshly ground black pepper

1 French-style baguette

¼ pound fresh goat cheese without rind, in one piece

8 ounces baby salad greens

»

Bake until cheese is soft and warm to the touch, 10 to 12 minutes.

While the cheese bakes, toss the salad greens with enough of the dressing to coat them lightly. Season with salt and pepper to taste and arrange on 4 plates. Toss the beets with some of the dressing and season with salt. (Toss red and golden beets separately.) Scatter the beets over the greens.

Divide the warm cheese among the 4 toasts, spreading it evenly. Garnish each salad with a cheese-topped toast.

Serves 4

My longtime friend Hallie Harron, now a chef in Arizona, shared this recipe for a cheese-friendly walnut bread. It is a moderately dense loaf with a nutty whole-wheat character, a generous lacing of toasted walnuts, and a subtle onion flavor. It would complement any fresh goat cheese or blue cheese, but Humboldt Fog is worth seeking out. Made by Cypress Grove Chèvre in McKinleyville, California, the cheese has a pure, vivid goat's-milk flavor, a creamy texture, and a thin layer of ash in the middle that makes it a beauty on a cheese tray.

1 cup walnuts

¼-ounce package active dry yeast (2½ teaspoons)

⅓ cup warm water (about 110°F)

1 cup milk

⅓ cup unsalted butter

About 3¼ cups unbleached all-purpose flour

½ cup whole-wheat flour

2½ teaspoons salt

⅓ cup minced shallots

2 tablespoons cornmeal

1 pound Humboldt Fog cheese

Alternative cheeses: Fourme d'Ambert, Morbier, Alsatian Munster, and Coach Farm goat cheeses

Preheat the oven to 350°F. Toast the walnuts on a baking sheet until fragrant and lightly colored, about 15 minutes. Let cool, then chop coarsely.

In a small bowl, sprinkle the yeast over the warm water and let stand for 2 minutes to soften, then whisk with a fork to dissolve. Let proof for 10 minutes.

In a small saucepan over low heat, heat the milk briefly, just until it is warm enough to melt the butter. Add the butter, remove from the heat and let the milk cool until it is just warm (about 110°F).

In a large bowl, stir together 1¾ cups of the all-purpose flour, the whole-wheat flour, and the salt. Add the proofed yeast, milk with butter, shallots, and walnuts. Stir vigorously until well blended. Add more all-purpose flour gradually, stirring until the dough becomes too stiff to stir. Turn out onto a lightly floured board and knead until the dough is smooth and elastic, about 5 minutes, adding more flour as necessary. If the walnuts pop out, poke them back in.

Shape the dough into a ball and transfer to a large buttered bowl. Turn to coat the surface with butter. Cover with plastic wrap and let rise until doubled, about 1½ hours. Punch the dough down and transfer to a lightly floured work surface. Reshape into a ball and transfer to a baking sheet dusted with the cornmeal. Cover with a towel and let rise until doubled, about 1½ hours.

Preheat the oven to 425°F. Put a baking dish filled with ice water on the floor of the oven to create steam. Slash the loaf in 3 or 4 places, then bake for 30 minutes. Reduce the oven temperature to 325°F, remove the baking dish of water, and continue baking until the bread is well browned and sounds hollow when tapped on the bottom, about 30 minutes more. Let cool completely on a rack before slicing.

Pass sliced bread with the wedge of cheese.

Makes one 8-inch round loaf

lentil salad with warm goat cheese

When I was a cook at Chez Panisse, the renowned Berkeley restaurant, many years ago, we often made a salad of dressed lentils with small clumps of soft goat cheese. This recipe is a variation, a warm lentil salad topped with a half-round of creamy baked goat cheese.

1 small round fresh goat cheese (about 5 ounces), chilled

¼ cup plus 3½ tablespoons extra-virgin olive oil

Scant ½ teaspoon coarsely cracked mixed peppercorns

1 cup lentils

1 teaspoon salt, plus more to taste

3 sprigs fresh thyme

½ cup finely minced celery

½ cup finely minced carrot

2 large cloves garlic, minced

¼ cup thinly sliced chives, plus more for garnish

1½ to 2 tablespoons red wine vinegar

Freshly ground black pepper

12 slices French-style baguette, cut on the diagonal

Using a piece of dental floss held taut between your hands, cut the goat cheese in half horizontally. Cut each half in half cross-wise to make half-moons. Put the 4 half-moons in a baking dish just large enough to hold them. Cover with 1½ tablespoons of the olive oil and the peppercorns.

Put the lentils in a saucepan and add cold water to cover by 1 inch. Add the salt and thyme sprigs and bring to a simmer over medium heat. Adjust the heat to a bare simmer and cook until the lentils are al dente, about 20 minutes. Drain and remove herbs.

While the lentils cook, heat 2 tablespoons of the olive oil in a small skillet over medium heat. Add the celery, carrot, and garlic and sauté until slightly softened, about 5 minutes.

In a bowl, combine the drained lentils, sautéed vegetables, remaining ¼ cup olive oil, ¼ cup chives, 1½ tablespoons vinegar, and salt and pepper to taste.

Preheat a broiler or toaster oven. Toast the baguette slices on both sides.

Reduce the oven temperature to 325°F. Bake the goat cheeses until they are warm and quiver when touched, 6 to 8 minutes. Divide the lentils among 4 plates. With a spatula, place a warm goat cheese on each mound of lentils. Top with a few sliced chives and a drizzle of oil from the baking dish. Put 3 toasts on each plate, or pass toasts separately. Serve immediately.

Serves 4

goat gouda with roasted hazelnuts and sherried figs

Aged goat's-milk Gouda from Holland has been a recent discovery for me but has quickly become a favorite. When just a few months old, the cheese is creamy white, smooth, and not terribly interesting. But with age, it deepens to a rich gold, with the texture of young Parmigiano-Reggiano and a sweet, nutty, almost caramel-like taste. For this recipe, ask your merchant for aged goat Gouda, anywhere from eighteen months to four years old. Pair it with a high-quality Spanish oloroso sherry, such as one from Lustau.

Note that you need to plump the figs one day ahead.

Remove the tough fig stems and cut the figs in half. Place in a small bowl and add just enough sherry to cover them. Cover the bowl and let stand at room temperature for 24 hours.

Preheat oven to 350°F. Toast the hazelnuts on a rimmed baking sheet until fragrant and lightly colored, about 15 minutes. Immediately wrap them in a kitchen towel and rub vigorously in the towel to remove as much of the skins as possible. (Some skin may adhere.)

Divide the cheese, hazelnuts, and figs among 6 plates and serve.

Serves 6

9 plump dried figs
Spanish oloroso sherry
48 hazelnuts
¾ pound goat Gouda

Alternative cheeses: Garrotxa, Manchego, Prince de Claverolle, Parmigiano-Reggiano, or Yerba Santa Shepherd's Cheese

cabécou with honey and walnuts

In southwest France, a *cabécou* (a colloquial word for "little kid") is a small, round disk of goat cheese—sometimes so small that one cheese makes a perfect single serving. The rounds range from fresh, soft, and mild (the best choice for this recipe) to well aged and hard. They are not widely available in the United States, so feel free to substitute another soft, young goat cheese. Gorgonzola would also be delicious presented this way.

If your honey has crystallized, set the jar in a small pan of water and heat gently until the honey liquefies.

The technique for removing the tannin from walnuts comes from Barbara Tropp's *Mastering the Art of Chinese Cooking.*

½ *cup walnuts*

½ *cup honey*

Four 1-ounce young Cabécou cheeses or other fresh, small goat cheese rounds

Alternative cheese: Gorgonzola

Put the walnuts in a small bowl and cover with boiling water. Let stand for 30 minutes, then drain and pat dry. Preheat the oven to 300°F. Line a heavy baking sheet with a triple thickness of paper towels. Put the walnuts on the paper towel–lined tray and bake for 30 minutes. Reduce the oven temperature to 250°F and continue baking until the walnuts taste completely dry inside, about 20 minutes more. Let cool.

In a small bowl, stir the walnuts into the honey. Put one Cabécou on each of 4 small plates. Spoon the walnut-honey mixture over the cheese, dividing it evenly. Serve immediately.

Serves 4

goat cheese platter with winter chicory salad

It's conventional, when composing a cheese platter, to present cheeses of different types: cheeses from cow's milk, from sheep's milk, and from goat's milk, for example. But good cheese counters today offer so much variety that it's possible to make a varied and inviting platter from goat's-milk cheeses alone. Like a wine enthusiast who might taste several Pinot Noirs side by side, you can better appreciate the possibilities open to the cheesemaker when you taste three decidedly different goat cheeses together.

Ask your cheese merchant for goat cheeses of varying styles: perhaps a young, fresh goat's-milk round from Coach Farm in New York, a nutty goat's-milk Gouda from Holland, or a firm Spanish Garrotxa, and an aged crottin from France or the extra-dry Yerba Santa Shepherd's Cheese (see Resources, page 104).

This salad and cheese platter would make an appealing cold lunch with bread, seasonal fruit, and a bottle of California Sauvignon Blanc, Italian Pinot Grigio, or French Sancerre or Vouvray. If I were serving it at the end of a dinner, I would pour a red wine—a Chinon or Bourgeuil from France or a California Cabernet Franc.

3 tablespoons walnut oil

1 tablespoon sherry vinegar

1 shallot, minced

Salt and freshly ground black pepper

½ cup walnuts

1 head frisée

½ large head radicchio

3 Belgian endives

¼ cup thinly sliced fresh chives

1 pound goat cheeses of three
  varieties

In a small bowl, whisk together the oil, vinegar, shallot, and salt and pepper to taste. Let stand for 30 minutes to allow the shallot flavor to mellow. Taste and adjust the balance as needed.

Preheat the oven to 350°F. Toast the walnuts on a baking sheet until fragrant and lightly colored, about 15 minutes. Let cool, then chop coarsely or break up by hand.

Use only the pale inner leaves of the frisée, reserving the darker outer leaves for another use. Tear the frisée into small pieces and place in a salad bowl. Core the radicchio and tear into bite-sized pieces; add to the bowl. Halve each endive lengthwise. Core, then cut crosswise into ½-inch pieces; add to bowl.

Add the chives, walnuts, and dressing to the chicories and toss to coat. Taste and adjust the seasoning. Divide the salad among 4 plates. Pass the goat cheeses separately.

Serves 4

baked goat cheese with warm red cabbage salad

Janet Tarlov, the cheese buyer for California's Oakville Grocery, shared this method of baking goat cheese with me. She coats the cheese with fine crumbs made from salad croutons, then broils the rounds to brown the crumbs. I find that the cheese needs a few more minutes in a hot oven, with the broiler off, to make it soft and creamy.

A Pinot Gris or Pinot Grigio (same grape, different names) would complement this salad. If you can only find 4- to 5-ounce rounds of goat cheese, cut them in half when cold—using dental floss held taut between your hands—to make individual portions.

Preheat the oven to 350°F. Toast the walnuts on a baking sheet until fragrant and lightly colored, about 15 minutes. Let cool, then break into small pieces or chop coarsely.

Heat 2 tablespoons of the olive oil in a 12-inch skillet over medium heat. Add the onion and sauté until just wilted, 3 to 5 minutes. Add the garlic and sauté for 1 minute to release its fragrance. Add the cabbage, fennel seed, 1½ tablespoons sherry vinegar, and salt and pepper to taste. Toss with tongs to blend. Cook briskly, stirring often, until the cabbage softens but still retains some crunch, 4 to 5 minutes. Taste and add a little more vinegar if desired. Add the walnuts and parsley. Transfer to a medium bowl to cool slightly.

Preheat the broiler and position a rack 7 to 8 inches from the heating element. Roll cheese in the remaining 1½ tablespoons olive oil, then in the crumbs, coating all sides evenly. (You may not need all the crumbs.) Place on a baking sheet and broil until the crumbs brown and crisp, 1 to 2 minutes. Reduce oven temperature to 425°F and bake the cheese until soft to the touch, 4 to 5 minutes.

Transfer the cheeses with a spatula to 4 individual plates. Divide the salad among the plates. Serve immediately.

⅓ cup walnuts

3½ tablespoons extra-virgin olive oil

½ large red onion, thinly sliced

1 large clove garlic, minced

½ small head red cabbage (about 12 ounces), cored and very thinly sliced

Scant ½ teaspoon fennel seed, coarsely crushed in a mortar or spice grinder

1½ tablespoons sherry vinegar, or more to taste

Salt and freshly ground black pepper

1 tablespoon chopped Italian parsley

Four 2-ounce portions fresh goat cheese without rind

½ cup fine crumbs made from homemade or storebought salad croutons

Serves 4

sheep's-milk cheeses

If there are more sheep's-milk cheese recipes in this book than the cheeses' popularity and availability might justify, it's due to my personal fondness for them. To my palate, most sheep's-milk cheeses have an appealing herbal taste and a pronounced acidity and sharpness, in contrast to the sweetness of cow's milk. Where cow's-milk cheeses often taste rich, nutty, and buttery, sheep's-milk cheeses tend to leave a leaner, cleaner, more focused impression.

Paradoxically, sheep's milk is considerably higher in fat than either cow's or goat's milk—although sheep's-milk cheese isn't necessarily higher in fat. A cheese's fat content depends largely on two factors: whether cream was added to the curd, as it is for double- and triple-crème cheeses; and how much water remains in the cheese. Hard, aged cheeses have a higher percentage of fat than many young, moist cheeses because the hard cheeses contain less water.

The salty sharpness of many sheep's-milk cheeses goes well with sweet fruit, such as watermelon, figs, quince, grapes, and cherries. In Spain, Manchego and quince paste are frequently paired. In Tuscany, it's pecorino and pears. These cheeses also have an affinity for many vegetables: Italians like to nibble fresh fava beans with young pecorino; Greeks scatter their lovely feta over cucumber-and-tomato salad; and, of course, we Americans crumble Roquefort in our green salads.

Sheep's-milk cheeses are among the few cheeses I like before dinner. Thin slices of Manchego with warm green olives (page 91) strike me as perfect cocktail food, as does a platter of Idiazábal with sliced fennel salami and orange oil (page 85). And after the meal, a slice of fresh sheep's-milk ricotta with summer fruit and homemade biscotti (page 76) makes a winning finale.

fresh sheep's-milk ricotta with peaches and pistachio-currant biscotti

At a summer picnic or lunch al fresco, serve fresh ricotta for dessert with the best farmers' market fruit and some small, crunchy biscotti. Sheep's-milk ricotta has a more compelling flavor, but cow's-milk ricotta will do. If you can't find dead-ripe peaches, substitute berries, apricots, cherries, or, later in the season, figs, apples, or pears. Serve the dessert with a knife and fork so that diners can spread the ricotta on the fruit. A sweet white wine or a sparkling wine would make a nice accompaniment. Store leftover biscotti in an airtight container.

PISTACHIO-CURRANT BISCOTTI

1/2 cup dried currants

1/2 cup warm water

1 1/2 cups shelled salted pistachios

2 cups all-purpose flour

1 1/2 teaspoons baking power

1/4 teaspoon salt

1/2 cup (1 stick) unsalted butter

1 cup sugar

2 eggs

2 teaspoons pure vanilla extract

1/2 teaspoon almond extract

1 tablespoon brandy

1 1/2 pounds sheep's-milk or cow's-milk ricotta

Sugar to taste

4 ripe peaches

To make the biscotti: Put the currants in a small bowl. Cover with the water and soak until softened, about 1 hour. Drain.

Preheat the oven to 325°F. Toast the pistachios on a baking sheet until fragrant and lightly colored, about 20 minutes. Let cool. Keep the oven on.

In a medium bowl, stir together the flour, baking powder, and salt.

In a mixer, cream the butter and sugar until light and fluffy, about 3 minutes. Add the eggs one at a time, beating well after each. Beat in the extracts and brandy. With the mixer on low, add the dry ingredients gradually, beating just until blended. Add nuts and drained currants and beat just until they are incorporated.

Line a heavy baking sheet with parchment paper. With 2 large spoons, transfer the dough to the baking sheet, making 3 logs about 14 inches long and 1 1/2 inches wide. The dough will be sticky. Shape the logs with the back of the spoons or with floured fingertips. Bake until the logs are firm to the touch and lightly colored, about 40 minutes. Let stand 15 minutes, then transfer to a cutting board and cut with a serrated knife into 3/8-inch-wide slices. Place the slices on an unlined baking sheet, cut side down, and bake until lightly colored and dry, 15 to 20

»

minutes. Transfer to a rack to cool. They will crisp as they cool.

At serving time, divide the ricotta among 8 individual plates. Top each portion with a sprinkling of sugar. Peel the peaches if desired. Slice and divide evenly among the plates. Put 2 or 3 biscotti on each plate.

Serves 8 (makes 7 dozen biscotti)

arugula salad with watermelon and feta

Lidia Kitrilakis, a food exporter in Greece, tells me that Greeks love feta with watermelon, especially at picnics. In more formal settings, such as restaurants, the fruit and cheese might be tossed with arugula to make a salad. Knowing how salt brings out the flavor in watermelon, I am not surprised that salty feta does the same.

Serve this refreshing salad in summer with charcoal-grilled chicken, pork, or lamb.

VINAIGRETTE

3 tablespoons extra-virgin olive oil

1 tablespoon lemon juice

1 shallot, minced

Salt and freshly ground black pepper

⅓ pound watermelon, trimmed of rind

6 ounces baby arugula or baby spinach

¼ pound Greek feta, crumbled

16 Kalamata olives

To make the vinaigrette: In a small bowl, whisk together the olive oil, lemon juice, shallot, and salt and pepper taste. Let stand for 30 minutes to allow shallot flavor to mellow. Taste and adjust the balance as needed.

Cut the watermelon into thin half-moon slices and remove the seeds, then cut the half-moons into roughly triangular pieces of manageable size.

In a large bowl, toss the arugula and watermelon with the dressing. Taste and adjust the seasoning. Transfer to a serving bowl or platter and top with crumbled feta. Scatter the olives around the edge of the salad. Serve immediately.

Serves 4

marinated feta with mint and capers

In Greece, cooks put up feta in large jars with pickled peppers, olives, and olive oil to flavor the cheese and extend its life. Here's a quicker version—an herbed marinade that penetrates the cheese in an hour. Take the feta on a picnic or serve it as a first course at a dinner al fresco with sliced tomatoes or roasted peppers, bread, black olives, and a bottle of rosé.

½ pound Bulgarian, Greek, or
    French feta

⅓ cup extra-virgin olive oil

1 large clove garlic, minced

¼ teaspoon red pepper flakes

1½ tablespoons chopped fresh mint

1 tablespoon chopped Italian parsley

1 generous tablespoon chopped
    capers

If the feta is in brine, drain and gently pat dry. Slice the cheese thinly, but try to keep each slice in one piece. Arrange the slices in a shallow dish just large enough to hold them.

In a small skillet, heat the olive oil with the garlic and pepper flakes over medium heat to release the fragrances, about 1 minute. Let cool completely. Stir in the mint, parsley, and capers. Pour over the feta. Marinate at room temperature for 1 hour, then serve directly from the dish.

Serves 4

baby spinach with shaved fennel and ricotta salata

Unlike fresh ricotta, which is soft and spoonable, salted ricotta *(ricotta salata)* has been pressed and aged until it is firm enough to slice. It is a specialty of southern Italy, often grated on tomato-sauced pasta or shaved over vegetables. I like it with sliced fresh tomatoes, with roasted peppers, with broccoli rabe—and with the raw spinach and thinly sliced fennel in this lemony salad. Serve as a first course and follow with grilled fish or shrimp, or serve after a seafood main course.

To make the vinaigrette: In a small bowl, whisk together the olive oil, 1 tablespoon of the lemon juice, garlic, and salt and pepper to taste. Taste the dressing and add more lemon juice if desired.

Cut off and discard the fennel stalks, if attached. Remove the outer layer of the bulb if it is bruised or thick and fibrous. Halve the bulb and thinly slice crosswise; you can do this by hand with a sharp knife, but a vegetable slicer, such as a mandoline, makes the task easier.

In a large bowl, combine the fennel and spinach. Add enough dressing to coat the greens lightly; you may not need it all. Toss gently. With a cheese plane, shave the cheese into the salad in thin slices. Toss gently. Taste and adjust the seasoning. Serve immediately.

Serves 4

VINAIGRETTE

3 tablespoons extra-virgin olive oil

1 to 1 1/2 tablespoons lemon juice

1 small clove garlic, minced

Salt and freshly ground black pepper

1 small bulb fennel

6 ounces baby spinach

3 ounces ricotta salata cheese

Alternative cheeses: Greek Manouri, feta (crumbled, not shaved), pecorino pepato, Sally Jackson's Sheep Cheese

When a meal is too rich to end with a full-scale cheese platter, I might serve salad tossed with a little cheese instead. Here's a favorite combination, a winter salad that delivers bitter and sweet, creamy and crunchy, in one mouthful. This pretty mix would also make an appealing light lunch.

3 tablespoons walnut oil

1 tablespoon white wine vinegar, or more as needed

1 shallot, minced

Salt and freshly ground black pepper

½ cup pecans

3 Belgian endives

1 bunch (about 6 ounces) watercress, about 3 loosely packed cups

⅓ pound seedless red grapes, halved

3 to 4 ounces Roquefort or other blue cheese

In a small bowl, whisk together the walnut oil, 1 tablespoon wine vinegar, shallot, and salt and pepper to taste. Let stand for 30 minutes to allow the shallot flavor to mellow. Taste and adjust the balance as needed.

Preheat oven to 325°F. Toast pecans on a baking sheet until fragrant and nutty, about 15 minutes. Let cool. By hand, break the pecans in half.

Cut each endive in half lengthwise and remove the core. Slice crosswise at 1-inch intervals.

In a large salad bowl, combine the endive, watercress, grapes, and pecans. Add enough of the dressing to coat the greens lightly; you may not need it all. Add the cheese, crumbling it by hand. Toss gently. Taste and adjust the seasoning. Divide among 4 salad plates or serve from the bowl.

Serves 4

On both the French and Spanish sides of the Pyrenees mountains, Basque shepherds make remarkable sheep's-milk cheeses. Road signs guide you to some of the farmhouses where cheeses are made and sold; other producers offer samples and sell their cheeses at simple roadside stands.

Fortunately, a growing array of these superb cheeses is available in the United States. Look for Ossau-Iraty, P'tit Basque, Etorki, Idiazábal, or others identified as Basque sheep's-milk cheese. On the French side of the mountains, the cheeses are often served with cherry or quince preserves; on the Spanish side, with quince paste *(membrillo)* or honey.

2 quince (about 1 pound)

1 cup sugar

¼ teaspoon cardamom seeds, crushed in a mortar or spice grinder

2 cups water

1 pound Pyrenees sheep's-milk cheese

Quarter, core, and peel the quince. Cut each quarter into 4 slices. In a medium saucepan, combine the sugar, cardamom, and water. Over moderate heat, bring to a simmer, stirring to dissolve the sugar. Add the quince, cover, and adjust the heat to maintain a gentle simmer. Cook until the quince are tender and rosy pink, about 2 hours. Let cool in the liquid, cover, then refrigerate.

Divide cheese and quince evenly among 8 individual plates.

Serves 8

idiazábal with fennel salami, olives, and orange oil

Made in Spain from raw sheep's milk, Idiazábal is a nutty, lightly smoked cheese that I find irresistible. Take it on a picnic or make it part of an antipasto with thinly sliced fennel salami, meaty olives, and a drizzle of fragrant orange oil. Basque chef Teresa Barrenechea, who owns Marichu restaurant in Manhattan, tells me that the Spanish Basque town of Ordizia has a juried Idiazábal contest, for which she has been a judge. The cheese is so beloved that people pay outrageous sums to taste the winner.

Remove the cheese rind if it is hard. (The rind on young Idiazábal may be soft enough to leave in place.) Thinly slice the cheese with a cheese plane or sharp knife. On a large platter, arrange the cheese slices on one side in a half-moon, the fennel salami on the other side, and the olives in the middle—or make any arrangement you like. Drizzle the cheese, salami, and olives with citrus oil, then serve.

Serves 4

Note: Check specialty-food shops for citrus oils—olive oils flavored with lemon, orange, blood orange, or tangerine. In many cases, the citrus is crushed along with the olives, producing an oil with a tantalizing citrus taste and fragrance. See Resources (page 104).

½ pound Idiazábal cheese

24 paper-thin slices of fennel salami

24 unpitted green olives, such as Picholine

Orange or other citrus oil (see Note)

Alternative cheeses: smoked mozzarella or San Simón (Spanish smoked cow's-milk cheese)

marinated pecorino with orange peel and herbs

This olive oil–steeped cheese is an adaptation of a recipe from Brian Streeter, the chef at Cakebread Cellars in the Napa Valley. The cheese should marinate for at least two days, but a longer stay won't hurt it. Look for a youngish pecorino that isn't too dry to slice and will absorb the marinade quickly.

This dish would be also be appealing with fresh pears or with sliced raw fennel. Use leftover oil—you will have a lot—as a dip for bread, or strain and use in vinaigrettes. Keep the leftover oil refrigerated.

Holding a knife parallel to the ends from which the rind was trimmed, slice the cheese into thin triangular pieces. You should get about 20 triangles from ½ pound of cheese.

Arrange the cheese in a dish just large enough to hold the slices in one layer. Scatter the pepper, bay leaves, rosemary, and orange zest evenly over the cheese. Cover completely with olive oil. Cover the dish with plastic wrap and refrigerate for 2 days. Remove from the refrigerator at least 4 hours before serving to allow the cheese to come to room temperature.

Divide the radicchio leaves among 4 plates, spooning a little of the seasoned oil and cracked pepper over them. Drizzle the leaves lightly with balsamic vinegar and sprinkle with salt. Arrange the cheese slices over or alongside the radicchio. Garnish each plate with a small cluster of grapes.

Serves 4

½ pound young pecorino toscano, in one wedge, rind removed

1½ teaspoons coarsely cracked black pepper

2 bay leaves, crumbled

2 teaspoons minced fresh rosemary

2 strips orange zest

1½ cups extra-virgin olive oil, or more as needed

12 to 16 outer leaves of radicchio

Balsamic vinegar

Kosher salt

⅓ pound red grapes

Alternative cheeses: Manchego, P'tit Basque, Toscanello, or Bellwether Farms' San Andreas

hearts of butter lettuce with fava beans and pecorino pepato

Sheep's-milk cheese and fresh, unpeeled fava beans are a common appetizer in Southern Italy. You peel the favas by hand and alternate tastes of sweet bean with salty cheese. For this salad, which brings the same ingredients together, look for a sheep's cheese studded with cracked black peppercorns—usually labeled pecorino pepato (peppered). Alternatively, use Spanish Manchego, Italian pecorino toscano, or another shaveable but pepperless sheep's-milk cheese, and season the salad with cracked black pepper.

VINAIGRETTE

3 tablespoons extra-virgin olive oil

1 tablespoon white wine vinegar

1 large shallot, minced

Salt and freshly ground black pepper

1 pound fava beans, shelled

2 heads butter lettuce

2 tablespoons minced Italian parsley

2 ounces pecorino pepato or
    Manchego

To make the vinaigrette: In a small bowl, whisk together the olive oil, vinegar, and shallot. Season with salt and pepper to taste. Let stand for 30 minutes to allow the shallot flavor to mellow. Taste and adjust the balance as needed.

Blanch the fava beans in a large pot of boiling water until tender (remove one, peel, and taste to be sure), 2 to 3 minutes. Drain and transfer to ice water to stop the cooking. Drain again. Remove outer skin, which should slip off easily.

Remove the outer green leaves from each head of butter lettuce until you reach the pale green heart. (Save the outer leaves for sandwiches or other uses.) Wash the hearts, tear the leaves into smaller pieces, and dry thoroughly.

In a medium bowl, toss the butter lettuce and 1 tablespoon of the parsley with all but 2 teaspoons of the dressing. Season with salt and pepper to taste. Divide leaves among 4 salad plates or arrange on a large platter. With a cheese plane, shave the pecorino into thin shards. Break up the shards by hand if large and scatter over the lettuce. Toss the fava beans with the remaining 2 teaspoons of dressing; season with salt and pepper to taste. Scatter the fava beans over the salad, then garnish with the remaining 1 tablespoon of parsley. Serve immediately.

Serves 4

sheep's-milk cheese with warm green olives

Just about any sheep's-milk cheese would be a compatible partner for these seasoned olives. Aged goat cheeses, such as Dutch goat Gouda or Spanish Garrotxa, would work well, too. The olives improve if made a day ahead. Let stand at room temperature, covered, and rewarm gently before serving with cocktails or the evening's first glass of wine.

With the side of a cleaver or large knife, gently smack the green olives to crack them; don't pound too hard or you will smash them.

Heat the olive oil in a small skillet over medium heat. Add the bay leaves, oregano, and fennel seed. Break the chile pepper in half and sprinkle some or all of the seeds into the skillet; add the chile pods to the skillet. Cook the seasonings briefly to release their fragrance, then add the olives. Cook, stirring, until the olives are hot throughout, about 2 minutes. Transfer to a small bowl and let stand until they are just warm.

Trim the cheese of any rind and cut into thin slices or small cubes. Place the cheese on one end of a serving platter and spoon the olives, with their seasonings, alongside.

Serves 6

1 cup unpitted green olives, such as Picholine

2 tablespoons extra-virgin olive oil

2 bay leaves, coarsely broken

½ teaspoon dried oregano

¼ teaspoon fennel seed, coarsely crushed in a mortar or spice grinder

1 dried red chile pepper

½ pound sheep's-milk cheese such as Idiazábal, P'tit Basque, or Manchego

sheep's cheeses with oven-dried tomatoes and toasted almonds

You don't need a special dryer to make these exquisite half-dried tomatoes, which are far more succulent and flavorful than the fully dried commercial varieties. After eight hours in a low oven, halved plum tomatoes will be wrinkled and shrunken but moist and intense, the flavor concentrating as water evaporates. Serve them with a selection of sheep's-milk cheeses—your choice, but aim for textural variety—and some toasted almonds.

If you are serving this cheese platter before dinner, pour a crisp Spanish fino sherry. If you are serving it after the main course, consider a richer oloroso sherry.

OVEN-DRIED TOMATOES

6 meaty plum tomatoes (about 1 pound), halved lengthwise

1 tablespoon extra-virgin olive oil

Salt

1 teaspoon dried herbes de Provence

TOASTED ALMONDS

1 cup whole unblanched almonds (about 5 ounces)

2 teaspoons extra-virgin olive oil

½ teaspoon kosher salt or sea salt

1 to 1¼ pounds sheep's-milk cheeses of two or three varieties, such as pecorino toscano, Manchego, Cabrales, Ossau-Iraty, Vermont Shepherd's Cheese, Old Chatham Pepper Pyramid, or Brin d'Amour

To make the tomatoes: Preheat oven to 250°F. Put the tomatoes in a nonaluminum baking dish. Drizzle with the olive oil. Season with salt to taste and the herbs, crumbling them between your fingers to release their fragrance. Bake until the tomatoes are very soft, wrinkled, and shrunken, but still moist, about 8 hours. Set aside to cool.

To make the almonds: Raise the oven temperature to 325°F. Bring a small saucepan of water to a boil over high heat. Add the almonds and blanch for 1 minute, then drain. Immediately transfer the nuts to a kitchen towel and wrap the towel around them. Vigorously rub the nuts in the towel to loosen the skins. Remove any skins that don't come loose; they should peel off easily by hand. Transfer the skinned nuts to a baking sheet. Rub with the olive oil and season with salt to taste. Bake until golden brown and fragrant, about 30 minutes. Transfer to paper towels to cool.

To serve, present the cheeses on a cheese board and pass the tomatoes and almonds separately. Alternatively, divide the cheeses, tomatoes, and almonds among 6 individual plates.

Serves 6

mixed-milk cheeses
and cheese platters

Although a single, perfect cheese can make a delightful cheese course, platters with multiple cheeses offer a chance to compare. For cheese lovers, there's something enormously appetizing about the sight of a tray with three or four selections and the knowledge that we don't need to choose: we can have some of each.

The guidelines for assembling cheese platters on page 11 should help you create appealing variety on your tray. In this chapter, I offer some examples of themed trays, showcasing favorite cheeses from several cheesemaking countries. By no means do you need a theme for your tray; a theme can give context to your selections and help you narrow your choices, but it doesn't ensure a successful assortment. I use these themes here merely as teaching tools, to introduce you to cheeses you might not know.

This chapter also includes a recipe for an autumn salad with Cabrales, a pungent Spanish blue cheese. Because the cheese may be made with a mixture of cow's, goat's, and sheep's milk, the recipe didn't comfortably fit anywhere else.

Lastly, I couldn't allow this book to end without offering a recipe for all those little bits of leftover cheese you are bound to accumulate. The French have the answer: *fromage fort* (page 103), an improvisational cheese spread that puts every remaining morsel to use.

american artisan cheeses with figs and field greens salad

Just what exactly is an artisan cheese? My dictionary doesn't even have a word that corresponds to the French *artisanal* or Italian *artigianale,* adjectives applied to foods made on a small scale, often by hand, and by someone who approaches his or her work as a craft, not as mass manufacturing.

Among the American cheeses that fit this definition and that would complement this fig salad are Laura Chenel's Taupinière, a fine aged goat cheese; Major Farm's Vermont Shepherd Cheese, reminiscent of the sheep's-milk cheeses of Basque country; and Great Hill Blue, a raw-milk cheese from Massachusetts and the finest American blue cheese I know. But you will find others at your favorite cheese shop. Choose two or three that will make a balanced cheese platter and serve them with this height-of-summer salad and some good bread.

To make the vinaigrette: In a small bowl, whisk together the oil, 1 tablespoon vinegar, shallot, and salt and pepper to taste. Set aside for 30 minutes to allow shallot flavor to mellow. Taste and adjust the balance, adding more balsamic vinegar if needed.

Preheat oven to 350°F. Toast walnuts until fragrant and lightly colored, about 15 minutes. Let cool. Break up any large pieces by hand.

Toss the greens and walnuts with vinaigrette. Add the figs and toss again gently. Taste and adjust the seasoning. Divide the salad among six plates, making sure the figs and walnuts end up on top. Pass the cheeses separately, or divide the cheeses among the six plates.

Serves 6

VINAIGRETTE

3 tablespoons extra-virgin olive oil

1 tablespoon balsamic vinegar, or
   more as needed

1 large shallot, minced

Salt and freshly ground black pepper

¾ cup walnuts

½ pound mixed field greens or baby
   lettuce mix

9 fresh figs, quartered

⅓ to ½ pound each of 3 American
   artisan cheeses (see introduction)

italian cheese trio with panforte

Dried fruits and nuts are classic cheese companions; in panforte, an Italian sweet, they come together in a dense, chewy, spicy confection. Serve thin wedges with a platter of Italian cheeses of varied character: a mild Gorgonzola dolce, an aged Parmigiano-Reggiano, and a Taleggio or Robiola, for example. To complement the panforte, I would pour a sweet wine such as Marsala, Italian *vin santo*, or Spanish oloroso sherry.

PANFORTE

1 cup hazelnuts

1 cup unskinned almonds

⅔ cup unbleached all-purpose flour

2 tablespoons unsweetened cocoa

2 teaspoons fennel seed, lightly crushed in a mortar or spice grinder

½ teaspoon cinnamon

⅛ teaspoon ground cloves

Grated zest of 1 orange

8 ounces dried Mission figs, thinly sliced (about 1½ cups)

⅔ cup sugar

⅔ cup honey

1½ pounds assorted Italian cheeses

Preheat the oven to 350°F. Toast the hazelnuts and almonds (together, if you like) on a rimmed baking sheet until fragrant and lightly colored inside, about 15 minutes. Let cool, then chop very coarsely. Reduce the oven temperature to 300°F.

Butter the bottom and sides of an 8-inch tart pan with a removable bottom or an 8-inch cake pan. Line the bottom with parchment paper and butter the parchment.

In a large bowl, stir together the flour, cocoa, fennel seed, cinnamon, cloves, and orange zest. Add the nuts and figs and stir to coat.

In a small saucepan, heat the sugar and honey over low heat, stirring until the sugar dissolves. Raise the heat to medium and cook, without stirring, until the mixture reaches 245°F on a candy thermometer, 2 to 3 minutes. Immediately pour over the nut mixture. Working quickly, stir until the dry ingredients are coated; the mixture will be stiff. Transfer to the prepared pan, spreading it evenly with a wooden spoon dipped in cold water. Bake for 40 minutes. The mixture will still be tacky to the touch. Cool the panforte completely on a rack, then remove from the pan and remove the parchment paper. Slice into 16 thin wedges.

Pass the cheeses and panforte separately.

Serves 8

One of the most unusual and memorable desserts I've ever encountered was served to me at Nuñez de Prado, a Spanish olive oil estate. For the final course in a meal designed to showcase the estate's extra-virgin oil, the kitchen sent forth a simple platter of honey- and oil-drizzled sliced oranges with almond pastries.

This blood orange salad contains no honey, but in its simplicity it comes close to my Nuñez de Prado memory. With it, offer three Spanish cheeses of varying texture and pungency: perhaps Garrotxa, Roncal, and the blue-veined Picón or Valdeon. If blood oranges aren't available, use navel oranges.

In a small bowl, whisk together the oil, shallot, and salt and pepper to taste. Let stand 30 minutes to allow shallot flavor to mellow.

Cut a slice off both ends of each orange so it will stand upright. Stand the orange on a cutting surface and, using a sharp knife, remove all the peel and white pith by slicing from top to bottom all the way around the orange, following the contour of the fruit.

Cut the peeled oranges crosswise into slices ¼ inch thick. Discard the first and last slices if they seem to be mostly membranes. Remove the small bit of white pith at the center of each slice. Arrange fruit on a platter or divide among 6 individual plates. Tear the mint leaves into small pieces and scatter over the orange slices. Spoon the dressing over the oranges, making sure the shallots are evenly distributed.

If you have arranged the oranges on a platter, serve cheeses separately from a cheese board. For an individual presentation, put a small portion of each cheese alongside the oranges on each plate.

¼ cup extra-virgin olive oil

1 large shallot, minced

Kosher salt and freshly ground black pepper

6 blood oranges

12 to 18 fresh mint leaves

1½ pounds Spanish cheese, of 3 varieties

Serves 6

three french cheeses with an apple, fennel, and walnut salad

So many cheeses would be compatible with this palate-refreshing salad, but here's one appealing trio: Reblochon, Valençay, and Fourme d'Ambert. Another option would be Cantal, Roquefort or Bleu de Gex, and Sainte-Maure.

Make the salad in fall and winter, when fennel and apples are at their crisp best.

5 tablespoons extra-virgin olive oil

2 tablespoons lemon juice

1 large shallot, minced

Salt and freshly ground black pepper to taste

¾ cup walnuts

2 large fennel bulbs

1 red apple, quartered and cored

3 tablespoons chopped Italian parsley

1½ pounds French cheese of 3 varieties

In a small bowl, whisk together the olive oil, lemon juice, shallot, and salt and pepper to taste. Let stand for 30 minutes to allow the shallot flavor to mellow. Taste and adjust the balance as needed.

Preheat the oven to 350°F. Toast the walnuts on a baking sheet until fragrant and lightly colored, about 15 minutes. Let cool, then break into small pieces by hand or chop coarsely.

Cut off and discard the fennel stalks, if attached. Remove the outer layer of the bulb if it is bruised or thick and fibrous. Halve the bulb and thinly slice crosswise; you can do this by hand with a sharp knife, but a vegetable slicer, such as a mandoline, makes the task easier. Cut the apple quarters crosswise into thin slices. In a large bowl, combine the fennel, apple, walnuts, and parsley. Add the dressing and toss well. Taste and adjust the seasoning.

Pass the salad and cheeses separately.

Serves 6

baby greens with persimmons, hazelnuts, and cabrales

Like so many other blue-veined cheeses, Spanish Cabrales has an affinity for winter fruits—pears, apples, oranges, dried fruits—and for nuts of all kinds. Heidi Krahling, the chef-owner at Insalata's in San Anselmo, California, brings all those components together in a salad of greens, Fuyu persimmons, Cabrales, and hazelnuts—a recipe she has kindly shared with me.

Merchants tell me that what is sold as Cabrales in this country is not always the real thing; often it's the milder Valdeón or Picón, both blue-veined cheeses from Asturias, the Spanish region that also produces true mixed-milk Cabrales. Because consumers tend to think any blue cheese from Spain is Cabrales (just as many think any blue cheese from France is Roquefort), the marketers have obliged by giving their cheese the more familiar name.

I am told that the authentic Cabrales exported to the United States today is wrapped in black foil, has many purplish-blue veins, and is extremely pungent. Valdeón and Picón are wrapped in leaves and are more approachable. Ask to taste at your cheese counter and buy the Spanish blue cheese you like best for this salad.

¼ tablespoon hazelnut or walnut oil

1 tablespoon plus 1 teaspoon sherry vinegar

1 large shallot, minced

Salt and freshly ground black pepper

¾ cup hazelnuts

1 large or 2 small Fuyu persimmons

1 large Belgian endive

⅓ pound mixed baby greens

¼ pound Cabrales cheese

In a small bowl, whisk together the oil, vinegar, shallot, and salt and pepper to taste. Let stand for 30 minutes to allow the shallot flavor to mellow. Taste and adjust the balance as needed.

Preheat the oven to 350°F. Toast the hazelnuts on a rimmed baking sheet until lightly browned and fragrant, about 15 minutes. Set aside to cool, then chop coarsely.

Peel and quarter the persimmons. Cut each quarter into thin slices.

Halve the endive lengthwise and core, then cut crosswise into thin half-rings.

In a large bowl, combine the greens, endive, and persimmons. Add just enough dressing to coat the leaves lightly; you may not need it all. Toss well. Taste and adjust the seasoning. Divide the salad among 6 plates. Crumble some of the cheese over each serving. Top with some of the hazelnuts.

Serves 6

If you regularly buy cheese, you can't help but amass little leftover chunks that are too small to serve but too big to throw away. When you can't see any other future for them, toss them in the food processor and make fromage fort ("strong cheese"), a pungent cheese spread that's appealing on warm toasts. You could serve it in a ramekin with before-dinner drinks, but I like to spread it on toasted baguette slices to accompany a green salad.

To my taste, fromage fort is always better when there's a little blue cheese in the blend. It will last for several days, refrigerated.

Remove any nonedible rind. If the cheeses are hard, grate them. Put all the cheese in a food processor with the garlic and 2 tablespoons white wine. Purée, adding more wine as needed to make a creamy, well-blended mixture. Add the brandy and purée again. Transfer to a ramekin. Use immediately, or cover and refrigerate, but bring to room temperature before using.

Makes 1 cup

½ pound assorted cheeses (weight after trimming)

1 small clove garlic, thinly sliced

2 tablespoons dry white wine, or more as needed

1 teaspoon brandy

resources

AMERICAN CHEESE SOCIETY
P. O. Box 303
Delavan, WI 53115-0303
414-728-4458
Fax: 414-728-1658
www.cheesesociety.com
The American Cheese Society is a
nonprofit organization dedicated
to encouraging the development
and appreciation of American-made
specialty cheeses.

THE CHEESE WORKS LTD.
2031-B Second Street
Berkeley, CA 94710
510-204-9736
Fax: 510-204-9731
The Cheese Works distributes
many of the imported and domestic
cheeses mentioned in this book.
If you are searching for a specific
cheese, call to inquire about a
retailer in your area that carries it.

For za'atar (page 59):
THE SPICE HOUSE
1941 Central Street
Evanston, IL 60201
847-328-3711
Fax: 847-328-3631

For fromage blanc direct-set culture
(page 60), high-quality cheesecloth,
and other cheesemaking needs:
NEW ENGLAND CHEESEMAKING
SUPPLY COMPANY
85 Main Street
Ashfield, MA 01330
413-628-3808
www.cheesemaking.com

For orange-flavored olive oil (page
85), Gorgonzola Mascarpone Torta
(page 38), and other hard-to-find
cheeses:
OAKVILLE GROCERY
7856 St. Helena Highway
Oakville, CA 94562
800-736-6602
www.oakvillegrocery.com

For Rubino's California mixed dried
fruit (page 35):
DEAN & DELUCA
607 S. St. Helena Highway
St. Helena, CA 94574
707-967-9980
www.deananddeluca.com

For Yerba Santa Shepherd's Cheese
(page 72):
YERBA SANTA DAIRY
6850 Scotts Valley Road
Lakeport, CA 95453
707-263-8131
This dairy's extra-dry goat's-milk
Shepherd's Cheese is aged at least
six months.

For Crescenza (page 26), San
Andreas (page 87), Pepato (page
88), and other superb cheeses:
BELLWETHER FARMS
9999 Valley Ford Road
Petaluma, CA 94952
888-527-8606
www.bellwethercheese.com

bibliography

These books were helpful to me in
preparing my manuscript.

Androuet, Pierre. *Guide du
Fromage.* U.K.: Aidan Ellis
Publishing, Ltd., 1983.

Ensrud, Barbara. *The Pocket Guide
to Cheese.* New York: Perigee Books,
1981.

Gayler, Paul. *A Passion for Cheese.*
New York: St. Martin's Press, 1997.

Jenkins, Steven. *Cheese Primer.* New
York: Workman Publishing, 1996.
A must-have reference for all cheese
lovers.

Teubner, Christian. *The Cheese
Bible.* New York: Penguin Studio,
1998.

index

pecorino toscano, marinated, with orange peel and herbs, 87
Peluso Cheese, 30
persimmons, baby greens with hazelnuts, Cabrales, and, 102
pistachio-currant biscotti, 76–78
prunes in red wine with Explorateur, 23
P'tit Basque, 84, 91
purchasing tips, 9–10

Quince, poached, Basque sheep's-milk cheese with, 84

Radicchio
    goat cheese platter with winter chicory salad, 72
    salad, Fontina Val d'Aosta with, 45
    Taleggio with Italian salad and hazelnuts, 37
ricotta, fresh
    baked, with parsley salad, 29
    with chestnut honey, chestnuts, and pears, 22
    sheep's-milk, with peaches and pistachio-currant biscotti, 76–78
ricotta salata, baby spinach with shaved fennel and, 81

Saint-André, 32
salads
    as accompaniments, 14
    apple, fennel, and walnut, French cheeses with, 100
    arugula, with watermelon and feta, 79
    baby greens with persimmons, hazelnuts, and Cabrales, 102
    baby greens with roasted beets and warm goat cheese toasts, 63–65
    baby spinach with shaved fennel and ricotta salata, 81
    blood orange, Spanish cheeses with, 99
    endive, with red grapes, pecans, and blue cheese, 82
    escarole and Gruyère, with walnut oil, 46
    field greens, American artisan cheeses with figs and, 97
    hearts of butter lettuce with fava beans and pecorino pepato, 88
    Italian, Taleggio with hazelnuts and, 37
    lentil, with warm goat cheese, 68
    mesclun and red pear, with triple-crème tartines, 32

mesclun with dried figs, blue cheese, and toasted almonds, 43
    parsley, baked ricotta with, 29
    radicchio, Fontina Val d'Aosta with, 45
    warm red cabbage, baked goat cheese with, 73
    winter chicory, goat cheese platter with, 72
salami, Idiazábal with olives, orange oil, and, 85
serving tips, 11
sheep's-milk cheeses, 75. See also individual varieties
    Basque, with poached quince, 84
    with oven-dried tomatoes and toasted almonds, 92
    with warm green olives, 91
Spanish cheeses with blood orange salad, 99
spinach, baby
    salad with watermelon and feta, 79
    with shaved fennel and ricotta salata, 81
Stilton with Port-glazed pears, 41
storage, 17–18

Taleggio with Italian salad and hazelnuts, 37
Teleme, homemade flatbread with truffle oil and, 30–31
tomatoes, oven-dried, sheep's cheeses with, 92
triple-crème cheeses, 32

Vella Dry Jack, Medjool dates, and toasted walnuts, 55
Vermont Cheddar with cranberry pear chutney, 51

Walnut bread with Humboldt Fog, 66–67
watermelon, arugula salad with feta and, 79

Yogurt cheese, Lebanese, with za'atar and olives, 59

Table of Equivalents

The exact equivalents in the following tables have been rounded for convenience.

oven temperature

FAHRENHEIT	CELSIUS	GAS
250	120	½
275	140	1
300	150	2
325	160	3
350	180	4
375	190	5
400	200	6
425	220	7
450	230	8
475	240	9
500	260	10

liquid and dry measures

U.S.	METRIC
¼ teaspoon	1.25 milliliters
½ teaspoon	2.5 milliliters
1 teaspoon	5 milliliters
1 tablespoon (3 teaspoons)	15 milliliters
1 fluid ounce (2 tablespoons)	30 milliliters
¼ cup	60 milliliters
⅓ cup	80 milliliters
½ cup	120 milliliters
1 cup	240 milliliters
1 pint (2 cups)	480 milliliters
1 quart (4 cups, 32 ounces)	960 milliliters
1 gallon (4 quarts)	3.84 liters
1 ounce (by weight)	28 grams
1 pound	454 grams
2.2 pounds	1 kilogram

length

U.S.	METRIC
⅛ inch	3 millimeters
¼ inch	6 millimeters
½ inch	12 millimeters
1 inch	2.5 centimeters